The Love of SOCCER

The Love of SOCCER

David Brenner

Foreword by Johan Cruyff

CRESCENT BOOKS
New York

Contents

End papers: **Sepp Maier, in goal for Bayern Munich, saves from the feet of Eintsacht Frankfurt's Bernd Holzentein in a** *Bundesligia* **match.**

Page one: **Nottingham Forest's Viv Anderson, the first black player to represent England at full international level. He is a stylish defender with a flair for attack.**

Page two-three: **Liverpool's Ray Clemence acclaimed as the best goalkeeper in the world today—few would dispute his standing.**

Page four-five: **Osvaldo Ardiles (white shirt, foreground), was a vital cog in Argentina's 1978 World Cup winning side and judged to be the best right-sided midfielder in the world.**

© **MCMLXXX Octopus Books Limited**
First published 1980 by Octopus Books Limited
59 Grosvenor Street, London W1

This edition is published by
Crescent Books, a division of Crown Publishers, Inc.

Brenner, David
Love of Soccer
1. Soccer. I. Title
GV943.B72   796.33'42 79-19341
ISBN 0.517.29624.1

Produced by Mandarin Publishers Limited
22A Westlands Road, Quarry Bay, Hong Kong

Printed in Hong Kong

Foreword

When I was invited to write the foreword to this book, I was first curious to know what the title would be. 'The Love of Soccer' was the answer, and it's a title I liked very much, because as a sport, soccer has always been my own great love and I can't think of anything that shows the international side of the game more than a Dutchman living in America contributing to a book written by an Englishman!

I can't count all the countries I've played in, either with Ajax, Barcelona, Los Angeles Aztecs and Washington Diplomats, or with the Dutch national side, but in each place I've visited, soccer has been, if you like, an international passport. I've made lots of good friends, both on and off the field, and I can't think of a sport other than soccer that would have allowed me to achieve all this. I'm pleased the book doesn't concentrate alone on the world's established teams and players because this is too often the case. It's good that attention is given to the younger players, because these are the stars of tomorrow, and also to the United States, for having played in that country, I think it could soon join the likes of Brazil, Argentina, Italy, West Germany, Holland and England as a real power in world soccer.

I'm sure that like me you'll be impressed by the scope and quality of the photographs and the words in this book and I'm sure too that it will only increase your own love of soccer.

Goalscorers and Goalkeepers

'Target men' versus 'custodians of the rigging'

Soccer is the most popular participant and spectator sport in the world today. With a pedigree that can be traced back not hundreds—as in some sports—but thousands of years, the game truly is one that cuts across all language and social barriers and its rules are the same from the lush turf of Wembley Stadium (the traditional 'home' of world soccer) to the tiniest municipal ground. At its best, soccer is about flair, artistry and imagination; at its worst, it is stereotyped, over-systemized, over-coached, and often violent both on and off the field.

In the first three chapters of this book, we shall be looking at the positive side of soccer: the players whose above-average ability in their own particular sphere of the game makes them just a little bit special. Where better to start than with the men who score goals and those whose prime task it is to stop them?

Thanks to the media, players who in past eras were simply known as 'Forwards' now enjoy a variety of glamorous-sounding titles. 'Strikers', 'Target Men', 'Front Runners' and 'Spearheads' are now-familiar labels used to describe those whose most important job in a side is to score as often and as efficiently as possible. Happily, goalkeepers have been spared the media's dubious attentions. No fancy titles for them, even in this modern age, though a turn-of-the-century newspaper report in England which described a goalie as 'the custodian of the rigging' might not have looked out of place in today's jargon-ridden soccer parlance.

Forwards against keepers is a fascinating contest as old as the game itself. Until quite recently, the laws of the game provided very little protection for the keeper in that they allowed him to be barged and buffetted by opposing players. This is no longer the case, but one country that suffered as a result of the change was England, where the 'traditional' centre-forward, a burly, tall, physically strong player, struck fear into the heart of many a Continental goalkeeper until well into the 1960s. None of these players was particularly creative —their sole job in life was to score often with either boot or head—but they were past masters at applying pressure, both physical and psychological, to opposing goalies.

Call it gamesmanship, kidology, or just plain cheating, but this pressure was remarkably effective—not so much in the domestic English game, where familiarity, to an extent, bred an increased awareness of the tricks of the trade, but

Previous page: **West Germany's Paul Breitner (no 3) watches anxiously as Sepp Maier goes down to save at the feet of Yugoslavia's Karasi. West Germany won this 1974 encounter 2–0, with Breitner scoring his country's opening goal during the first half.**

Below: **Watched by team-mate Tony Currie (red shirt, centre), England's Kevin Keegan slams home a free kick to score in the international played at Wembley against Brazil in 1978. Keegan was named European Footballer of the Year in 1978 and 1979, only the second player after Johan Cruyff to win the award in successive years.**

Left: **Italy's Paolo Rossi (blue shirt), who was one of the most successful forwards in Argentina, evades a tackle from Hungary's Sandor Pinter as Tibor Rab looks on. The scoreboard in the background shows Italy to be leading 2–0; Rossi scored the game's first goal after 35 minutes and Italy ran out comfortable 3–1 winners.**

particularly when an English side, either at international or club level, played a foreign team. Opposing goalies, nurtured on tales of beefy English centre-forwards, developed the unfortunate habit of letting their concentration lapse by keeping one eye on the ball and the other on the supposed English 'villain' and, too often for it to be merely coincidental, their performance suffered as a result. So English centre-forwards acquired something of a legendary status, from Bill 'Dixie' Dean, scorer of 60 League goals in the 1927/8 season (a record that still stands), through Nat Lofthouse, nicknamed the 'Lion of Vienna' after his performance in England's 3-2 win over Austria in 1952; Tommy Lawton, perhaps the finest header of the ball ever; to Bobby Smith, a stalwart for Tottenham and England during the early 1960s; and finally to Geoff Hurst, the only man ever to score a hat-trick in a World Cup Final, a feat he achieved during England's 4-2 win over West Germany in 1966.

Perhaps in order to combat the physical presence of centre-forwards like these, English goalkeepers over the years developed the physical side of their own game and so have always somehow seemed a breed apart to their foreign counterparts. Traditionally, the English game has always had a wealth of goalkeeping talent and names like Frank Swift and Gordon Banks come readily to mind. Currently in Peter Shilton of Nottingham Forest, Ray Clemence of Liverpool and Manchester City's Joe Corrigan, England has three goalkeepers who would walk into all but a handful of international sides. To their names add West Ham's Phil Parkes,

whose transfer from Queens Park Rangers for £500,000 ($1,000,000) in 1978 made him the world's most expensive keeper, and youngsters like Chris Woods and Gary Bailey and you get some idea of England's strength in depth. Scottish, Welsh and Irish goalies don't seem to have the same sort of consistency, for some reason, although there are of course honourable exceptions, not least of whom is Northern Ireland's Pat Jennings, now into his thirties but performing as well as ever for Arsenal after a record-breaking career at Tottenham.

If England can lay claim to half-a-dozen or so top-flight goalkeepers to illustrate the richness of the talent available, good foreign keepers are rare indeed by comparison. The names that instantly come to mind are Italy's Dino Zoff, Sepp Maier of West Germany, Ubaldo Fillol of Argentina, Leao of Brazil, Sweden's Ronnie Hellstroem and, arguably, Jan Tomaszewski of Poland. Too often, though, foreign keepers excel at the spectacular, but are technically unsound, so perhaps it is the reliability of the English goalie which, when added to skill, courage and temperament, makes him the best in the world.

While England has almost an embarrassing excess of star goalies, the same cannot be said for their forwards. As early as 1953, the Hungarian centre-forward Hidegkuti gave a glimpse of what was to come, playing a deep-lying game in the side that thrashed England 6-3 at Wembley and then repeated the dose with a 7-1 win in Budapest six months later. In the great Real Madrid side of the fifties, Alfredo di Stefano took the art of centre-forward play to sublime heights,

adding subtlety, scope and immense ball skills to the other traditional goal-scoring values. The English game meanwhile, blind almost to the point of lunacy, ignored modern Continental trends in forward play which discarded the traditional centre-forward for a more mobile, though no less penetrative, player. So from the late 1960s onwards England has increasingly lagged behind the rest of the world in terms of forward play, persisting with the old-fashioned type of centre-forward when, as far as the world's best like Holland, West Germany, Italy and Brazil are concerned, the breed no longer has a real place in the game.

Modern centre-forward perfection is shown by players like West Germany's Gerd Muller, the scorer of 68 goals in 62 international appearances. The majority of Muller's goals, both for West Germany and for his club Bayern Munich, were close-range efforts which led to criticism (entirely unjustified), that he was nothing more than a 'goal poacher'. Such a view belittles a highly-talented player. Muller's attributes were a devastating turn of speed over 5 yards (5 metres), lightning reflexes, great positional sense, coolness and a deadly finish with either head or foot; in short, the ideal qualities needed to score goals in an era of packed defences and half-chances.

Now that Muller has retired from the European game to seek his fortune in America, perhaps the best new-style centre-forward is Hans Kranki of Austria and Barcelona. In 1977, he scored six goals in Austria's 9-0 drubbing of Malta in a World Cup qualifier and once in Argentina he scored four goals (including one penalty) in six games—a total only surpassed by Mario Kempes' six goals for Argentina and the five apiece of Holland's Robbie Rensenbrink (four of them penalties), and Peru's Teofilio Cubillas (two penalties). Transferred to Barcelona from Austria Wien after the World Cup finals, Krankl became Spain's top scorer in his first season and completed a marvellous year for him by scoring one of Barcelona's goals in the 4-3 win over Fortuna Dusseldorf that gave them the 1979 European Cup-Winners Cup.

If the 'traditional' centre-forward is an anachronism in the modern game, the 'traditional' winger is enjoying something of a come-back. It's unquestionably true to say that with the unique dribbling skills of Stanley Matthews, England 'gave' wingers to the rest of the world—and until 1966, the pupils learnt their lesson well, with players like Gento of Real Madrid and Garrincha of Brazil taking the art of wing-play to new heights. The year 1966 marked the temporary end of the winger whose sole task in life was to stay within 2 yards (2 metres) of the touchline to collect passes from midfield and defence before scooting down to the goal-line at the greatest possible speed before crossing the ball into the goalmouth or laying it back. In that year, however, England won the World Cup with an innovatory 4-3-3 formation in which wingers played no part. Instead, the task of giving width to the attack was given to the full-backs, whose penetrating runs down the wings, added of course to their defensive abilities, made them more complete players than 'mere' wingers alone.

Since the cliché about imitation being the sincerest form of flattery probably holds truer in soccer than anywhere else, England's 1966 World Cup success instantly led to a plethora of winger-less 4-3-3 line-ups at international and club level the world over. Of course, wingers didn't obligingly disappear from the scene. Most sides continued to play one winger in attack, but the days when the winger's domain was the touchline alone were gone. Now the winger was given a more mobile, free-ranging role, switching from flank to flank in an effort to unsettle defences with speed and control. Instead of being just feeders of the ball into the penalty area, wingers were now encouraged to cut in and go for goal themselves.

In the wayward talents of George Best, Britain had one of the greatest wingers of all time and at varying periods during the 1970s, Dragan Dzajic of Yugoslavia, Robert Gadocha of Poland, Dominique Rocheteau of France, and Scotland's Willie Johnstone and John Robertson, together with Russia's Oleg Blokhin, have all shown that the winger has a place in any forward line. Indeed, the England team of the past couple of years has played regularly with two wingers —Steve Coppell and Peter Barnes—thus neatly taking the trend full-circle: but with one major difference. The 'old' wingers of the 1950s and early 1960s has hardly any defensive

responsibilities, but in England's two-winger formation, the 'new' wingers Barnes and Coppell are expected to cover back if necessary. So whereas the England team of 1966 had full-backs acting as wingers, the England side today has wingers if not quite acting as full-backs, then at least assuming a far bigger role in midfield and defence than their predecessors did.

Though the part played in the game by wingers and centre-forwards has altered over the past couple of decades, at least the position of the inside-forward has remained relatively stable. Their function in a side, broadly speaking, is either to score goals or to create them. Of course, creative inside-forwards like Trevor Brooking of West Ham and England often score goals and goalscorers like Mario Kempes of Valencia and Argentina can be creative, but the men who can do both with equal effectiveness are a rare breed. The incomparable Pele was one, Johan Cruyff another. Arguably Kevin Keegan of Southampton and England can be placed

in that category too. Any reason for argument would not arise because of doubts concerning Keegan's ability, because *currently* he's almost certainly the most accomplished all-round player in the world, but because his role in a side—as regards England, at any rate—has often been difficult to define.

Although originally an out-and-out winger, his style of play was changed during his time at Liverpool and became less and less orthodox. He has played in midfield, but at his most effective he is a deep-lying attacking player, often prompting moves and often scoring, too. Although pigeon-holing players is at best rather a futile task, Keegan does seem to fit into the goal scoring/creative slot so loftily occupied by both Pele and Cruyff. As regards purely goal-scoring inside-forwards, Kempes made his mark in the 1978 World Cup finals with six goals—all from open play—in seven games, a feat that rightly led to him winning the Golden Ball award as the best player in the tournament.

Second to Kempes in the World Cup awards was Italy's Paolo Rossi—a player of immense future promise—and third was Dirceu of Brazil, who came to Argentina very much in the shadow of Zico, a player heralded before the tournament began as 'the white Pele'. In fact, Zico turned out to be no such thing and had a thoroughly forgettable World Cup, scoring only one goal (and that from a penalty) and eventually being dropped for Brazil's last game—the third-place play-off against Italy. Dirceu, on the other hand, seemed to improve with every game in Argentina and had the satisfaction of scoring Brazil's winning goal against Italy.

For all his brilliance, Pele has left Brazil with rather an unfortunate legacy, for whenever a young forward with a little bit more flair than normal appears on the domestic scene, he is immediately dubbed 'the new Pele', which is unfair on the youngster and on the unique talents of Pele himself. The current 'new Pele' in Brazil is Socrates, an extremely gifted young black forward who plays for the

Far left: **Although hailed as 'the white Pele', Zico had a disappointing World Cup for Brazil in 1978 and ended up being dropped from the international side. Now, however, he seems to have recovered his zest for the game and is once more an established Brazilian international who will probably appear in the 1982 World Cup.**

Left: **Hans Krankl is one of Austria's most prolific goal-scorers ever and is equally successful with his club—the Spanish First Division side Barcelona. Fast and skilful despite his size, Krankl is equally adept both in the air and on the ground.**

Centre: **West Germany's Gerd Muller was without question the most lethal international goal-scoring machine of modern times. In 62 appearances for his country, he scored 68 goals (a record that even the great Pele cannot equal), including the winner in the 1974 World Cup.**

Above: **In the author's view, Holland's Johan Cruyff is the greatest all-round player in soccer history, equally adept in midfield or attack and with the arrogant skills to turn the tide of matches single-handedly. After a two-club European career with Ajax Amsterdam and Barcelona, he now plays for Washington Diplomats.**

Corinthians club in the Sao Paulo section of the Brazilian championship. With Zico now recovered from his failure in Argentina and once again scoring goals for his club Flamengo (including six in a 7-1 win over Goytacaz in a Rio championship game in mid-1979), a Socrates-Zico partnership in the Brazilian attack might one day be a familiar sight in the international soccer arena.

World champions Argentina too have discovered a player to whom they refer as 'the Argentinan Pele'. He's Diego Maradona, a precocious teenager who plays for the Argentinos Junior club in Section A of his country's Metropolitan First Division. 'Unveiled' during Argentina's European tour during the summer of 1979, he played with a poise that belied his years and comparative international inexperience and scored some tremendous goals. One goal in particular stunned the Hampden Park crowd into disbelieving silence during Argentina's 3-1 win over Scotland, such was the acuteness of the shot's angle and the almost disdainful way with which Maradona took his time before shooting, practically turning the entire Scottish defence inside-out. Indeed, Argentina now seem to have three world-class inside-forwards at their disposal in the shape of Kempes and Maradona and also in Leopoldo Luque, Kempes' forward partner in 1978, who himself scored four times during those epic finals and would probably have had more but for a leg injury that kept him out for two games.

From Britain's viewpoint, there are currently two players in the game, both on the brink of establishing themselves as long-term internationals and cementing a claim for world recognition. The first is Trevor Francis, British soccer's first million pound player, who in addition to helping his new club Nottingham Forest to the 1979 European Cup has also won a vast number of admirers in America with his goal-scoring feats for Detroit. Francis has already played for England and shows signs of developing what could be a very potent partnership with Kevin Keegan. The second is Scotland's Andy Gray, a centre-forward in the 'new' mould, who would certainly have been first choice for his country in Argentina but for a depressing run of injuries that kept him out of the tournament. In 1977, Gray's fellow professionals in the English Football League not only voted him 'Young Player of the Year' but also 'Player of the Year' overall, a tribute to his current standing in the game and to his future potential.

Left: **It might be hair-raising for Liverpool's Phil Thompson, but his team-mate Ray Clemence seems to have the situation well in hand. In the background, Alan Hansen holds a watching brief. Liverpool's defence in depth—as amply demonstrated here—is one of their great trademarks. Liverpool dominated the British club scene to an astonishing degree over the last decade which included two European cup victories.**

Above: **Perhaps the most exciting young player in the world at present is Argentina's Diego Maradona (striped shirt), seen here leaving a trail of Dutch defenders in his wake during the Argentina v Holland game played during 1979 to commemorate FIFA's 75th anniversary. Holland, who also produce such inspired players, have been eclipsed in international football over the last few years.**

2

The World's Midfielders

The skills of creative play

To say that games are won and lost in midfield may be the oldest soccer cliché there is, but it is nevertheless the truest of statements. Brazil won the 1958 World Cup with a 4-2-4 formation—in other words, with a two-man midfield line-up. In 1966 England pioneered 4-3-3. And in 1978 Argentina gave us a formation that was midway between 4-2-4 and 4-4-2, but with stronger shades of the latter as Kempes and Luque were the only out-and-out attackers, while the two wingers Ortiz and Bertoni struck from midfield positions. The trend then over the past 20 years has been for the midfield to become more and more congested and the reason for this is a fear of losing, such are today's rewards for success.

Two players in midfield, such as Brazil fielded in 1958, are relatively easy to mark out of the game, thus making for a vacuum between defence and attack. A three-man midfield is harder to mark and a four-man midfield harder still. The reasoning is that the more players a side has in midfield, the more ball possession it will win and the more goal chances will be created. Unfortunately, the practice belies the theory, for when two teams playing a 4-4-2 formation meet each other the result is eight players contesting for the ball in an area extending roughly 25 yards (25 metres) either side of the halfway line. No wonder, then, that creative play tends to get stifled and the accent is placed far too often on safety-first percentage soccer, keeping possession and waiting for opponents' errors. But, as the role of centre-forwards and wingers has been adapted to the needs of the modern game, so too has that of the midfield creator, for although goal-scoring players most frequently grab the headlines, their midfield partners are in a sense more valuable to the side.

Occupying a midfield as opposed to an out-and-out attacking role, the modern creative inside-forward was in a sense 'born' during the 1966 World Cup, when Martin Peters,

Previous page: **Maszczyk of Poland (no 14, red strip) throws up a shower of spray as he slides in to tackle West Germany's Wolfgang Overath during a vital World Cup match between the two countries in 1974. Back-up men in the shape of Domarski (red shirt) and Schwarzenbeck (white shirt) are both ready to lend a hand if needed.**

Left: **Not even his greatest admirers would claim that Alan Ball is still among the world's top midfielders. But his boundless energy and enthusiasm made him a world class member of England's World Cup sides in 1966 and 1970 and although now in the veteran stage, he helped Vancouver Whitecaps to their 1979 Soccer Bowl win.**

judged ten years ahead of his time by England team manager Sir Alf Ramsey, gave a sublime display of midfield creative skills added to his ability of 'ghosting' into goal-scoring positions. The style of play pioneered by Peters was continued at his club, West Ham, and also in the England side by Trevor Brooking, who is now at the very peak of his career and on his day is perhaps the best left-sided midfield player in the world. The best right-sided midfielder the world has to offer is probably Osvaldo Ardiles, a vital cog in Argentina's World Cup-winning side. Now with Tottenham Hotspur in the English First Division, Ardiles confounded the critics who maintained that a player of his delicate style and slight physique would simply be swamped by the sheer physical pressures (not to mention the heavy, cloying mid-winter pitches) of the English game. However, his first season in this alien environment proved an unqualified success and went some way towards showing that a great player, as Ardiles is, can perform under almost any conditions.

With some slight variations, virtually every domestic and international side in the world today now plays either 4-3-3 or 4-4-2 and since the midfield is the busiest place on the pitch, players in midfield positions are consequently more involved in the game and see more of the ball than their team-mates in defence and attack. Basically, midfield players can be placed in one of two distinct categories. On the one hand, there are the sheer creators like Brooking and Ardiles who set up attacks. On the other, there is the ball-winner whose job it is to get possession of the ball and then feed his creative players.

The ball-winners in today's game are the dynamos driving the rest of the side. Full of strength, courage and the ability to work for a full 90 minutes each and every game, the modern ball-winner's lineage can be traced back to Duncan Edwards of Manchester United, whose career came to a tragically early end when he was killed in the 1958 Munich Air Disaster which wiped out virtually half the United side, then one of the very best in Europe. Although he was only 21 years old when he died, Edwards was already an established England international. He had 18 appearances to his credit, together with six caps for the Under-23 side for whom he first played when he was just 17, a year after his League debut with United and a year before he was selected for the full England side as the youngest player before or since to gain selection. His style was pure power and if Martin Peters was indeed 10 years ahead of *his* time, then Duncan Edwards played 20 years too soon, for in the type of soccer that's played today he would have been quite simply unstoppable. Not only could he tackle like a demon but he could also distribute the ball thoughtfully and accurately and was never afraid to thunder upfield in support of the attack—as was

demonstrated by the many goals struck with fearsome power from long range.

The style of midfield play pioneered by Edwards flourished in the English game to the extent that until very recently, the ball-winner was an established fixture in the international side. Nobby Stiles, whose uncompromising tackling made him a target for referees and opposing fans alike, performed the task in England's 1966 World Cup side and he was followed by a succession of players like Alan Mullery and Norman Hunter who excelled in the ball-winning role allotted to them. During the 1970s, Liverpool's Emlyn Hughes (in style, a similar sort of player to Edwards) performed the task before dropping back into a more defensive role, while in Gerry Francis, England had a captain who would still be an international had not a succession of knee injuries curtailed his career. In fact, England's current international decline can be put down to—among other factors—the present lack of such a player, for without such support in midfield, the creative players, who are never particularly strong tacklers, simply don't see enough of the ball.

Scotland has also produced some notably aggressive ball-winning players. In the 1960s, Dave Mackay, the captain of Scotland, came from the Edinburgh club Heart of Midlothian to establish himself in the Tottenham side that in 1961 became the first this century to complete the League and FA Cup 'Double'. Mackay's commitment to the game can best be summed up by his achievement of overcoming two breaks of the same leg (injuries that would spell the end of a career for most players) to captain Tottenham to their FA Cup win over Chelsea in 1967.

In the same mould as Mackay was Billy Bremner, a player now in the twilight of his career, who was in the all-conquering Leeds United side of the late 1960s and early 1970s along with Norman Hunter. Bremner, fiery and red-headed, was frequently in trouble with referees for his abrasive style, although his clashes with officialdom were more the result of having let his enthusiasm get the better of him than for a questionable style of play. Like Mackay, he captained Scotland and like Mackay again, he won virtually every honour that the game in Britain has to offer.

On the Continent, one of the fiercest tacklers in the game is Romeo Benetti of Italy, whose close-marking abilities and general all-round skill make him a player of genuine world stature. On a par with Benetti are the Dutch pair of Johan Neeskens and Arie Haan, for so long the backbone of their national side, although neither has played Dutch league soccer for some time. Haan is with the Belgian club Anderlecht, while Neeskens has perhaps put his international career in jeopardy by joining New York Cosmos of the North American Soccer League after a spell with Barcelona. Both Haan and Neeskens are something of a rarity: not only are they fine ball-winners, but they also have excellent distribution and can score a useful number of goals each season. Indeed, it was Haan who scored one of the best goals of the 1978 World Cup finals, a screamer from fully 30 yards (30 metres) out in the game against Italy that gave Holland a 2-1 win.

In terms of formations open to managers and coaches, as regards the basic 4-3-3, the ideal midfield combination would be along the lines of a creative passer of the ball like Ardiles or Brooking; a tough/tackling ball-winner like Benetti; and finally, shaping the midfield trio into a cohesive unit, a player capable of holding the ball and speeding up or slowing down play as necessary—a sort of onfield tactical director, in loose terms maybe the equivalent of the quarterback in American football. Kevin Keegan, when playing in a midfield role, is very adept at this skill, as was Franz Beckenbauer on the occasions he forsook his defensive duties and moved forward. So too was Johan Cryuff when playing deep.

Although 4-3-3 is basically an attack-orientated formation, the more recently introduced 4-4-2 places more emphasis on defence, particularly if the 'extra' midfield man is used

primarily as an aid to the back four. At its best, 4-4-2 is an undeniably effective line-up, for if the midfield players have the capability, they can not only establish an iron grip on the vital central area of the game, but also push up in support of the attack and defend in depth.

Perhaps the best example of this was Liverpool's 4-4-2 system during their two years as European champions in 1977 and 1978. In 1977 against Borussia Moenchengladbach in the European Cup Final, the Liverpool midfield comprised Kennedy, Case, McDermott and Callaghan, while in the 1978 Final against FC Bruges, apart from the inclusion of Graeme Souness in preference to Callaghan, the same players again occupied the midfield positions. In this Liverpool side, the two ball-winners were Terry McDermott and Jimmy Case, while Souness and Kennedy took over the holder/passer responsibilities. Where Liverpool were so fortunate was that all four midfield players could and did score goals on a regular basis in addition to being prepared to drop back and help out the defence whenever the need arose.

On the creative front, we have already considered Osvaldo Ardiles and Trevor Brooking as the best players in their own particular sphere at present, but not far behind is Italy's Franco Causio. Like Ardiles, he is a right-sided player, but his attacking and creative instincts are often blunted by his withdrawn positioning in the Italian national side.

No such problems surrounded Gunter Netzer of West Germany during the height of his career, however. English soccer fans have particular cause to remember the impact made by Netzer when the two countries met in a European Nations Cup-tie at Wembley in 1972. Germany won 3-1 and their success was almost entirely due to Netzer's total dominance of midfield. Time and again he gathered the ball in his own half to swoop down on the England defence before laying the ball off to his attackers and his form throughout that particular tournament helped guide West Germany to eventual victory in the Final against Russia. Often a partner of Netzer's was Uli Hoeness of Bayern Munich, a versatile player adept in attack but most effective in midfield. His was the dominant midfield role in West Germany's 1974 World Cup triumph when, with his midfield partners Rainer Bonhof and Wolfgang Overath, he was successful in wresting control of the game from the equally fine Dutch midfield trio of Neeskens, Van Hanegem and Jansen—Arie Haan on this occasion was preferred in defence. As a blend suited to the requirements of their own national sides (in Holland's case feeding Cruyff; in West Germany's, Muller), the Dutch and West German midfields in that particular game couldn't really have been bettered by any other line-up in the world.

Of those six players, Overath—who played in the 1966

Left: **Carefully watched by Mario Kempes (with moustache), and Osvaldo Ardiles (no 2), France's Michel Platini prepares to lay the ball off during the 1978 World Cup match between the two countries. Argentina won 2–1, but Platini had the satisfaction of scoring his country's goal.**

Below: **The powerful running of West Germany's Uli Hoeness sweeps him past this challenge from Poland's Kaziu Deyna (red shirt, left) and Domarski. Now retired from active soccer, Hoeness is still with his *Bundesligia* club Bayern Munich as general manager, while his brother Dieter carries on playing.**

Final against England—has now retired and so has Hoeness, while Bonhof has left his German club Borussia Moenchengladbach and is now a team-mate of Mario Kempes' with Valencia. Of the Dutch, Neeskens and Jansen again occupied midfield berths during the 1978 World Cup Final, while Van Hanegem, absent in 1978, now plays in the North American Soccer League.

You don't necessarily have to be Dutch to feel huge pangs of sympathy for Neeskens, Jansen and Haan (who moved from defence in 1974 to his more favoured midfield position in 1978) for the cruel manner in which fortune has treated them, because while they were up against one of the best current midfields in the Final against West Germany, the same fate befell them four years later. In 1978, Argentina fielded only two recognized midfield players—Ardiles and Gallego—although the wingers Ortiz and Bertoni frequently dropped back into midfield when Holland were attacking. This midfield strength in depth gave the eventual world

champions a marginal edge in midfield that was ultimately to prove decisive.

Scotland would probably have fared better in Argentina had their then-manager Ally McLeod played the midfield formation that the prevailing conditions and form (or in the case of some players, lack of form) demanded. Scotland has always been rich in skilled midfield creators and the six midfielders in their 1978 World Cup squad were as good as any in the tournament. However, McLeod opened with a 4-3-3 formation that proved totally ineffective; swapped players, but still kept to 4-3-3, for a second disastrous game and only changed to 4-4-2 too late in the day for it to have any effect. That his final selection resulted in a 3-2 win over Holland provided an aftertaste of what might have happened had that particular midfield of Rioch, Gemmill, Hartford and Souness been utilized right from the start.

As for England, despite the brave single-mindedness of manager Ron Greenwood in persisting with a 4-2-4/4-4-2

line-up throughout 1978 and 1979 without really getting the results he wanted, the short term is pretty bleak, but the long term is infinitely brighter. During 1978/9, the England team operated with only two recognized midfield players—Brooking and Manchester United's young Ray Wilkins, neither of whom are competitive ball-winners. From time to time, Tony Currie of Queens Park Rangers was given an outing in midfield, but although he is a more forceful player than either Brooking or Wilkins, in style and appearance very like Gunter Netzer, he is not a specialist ball-winner either. Another midfielder called sporadically into the England side was Liverpool's Terry McDermott, another player very much in the Currie mould, but again not a particularly strong tackler. As a result, England turned in some stuttering performances during the period, relying heavily on the excellence of the defence not to concede too many goals and the brilliance of Kevin Keegan, who got through a prodigious amount of work both in midfield and attack.

With added aggression in midfield, there's no doubt at all that the England side would be a more than useful one. Although Brooking might not be around when the 1982 World Cup finals are held in Spain, Wilkins almost certainly will be, as will two more of England's brightest young hopes of the moment, Tottenham's elegantly gifted Glenn Hoddle and the ebullient Gary Owen of West Bromwich Albion.

Wales (despite some sterling successes in the European Championship) and Northern Ireland can be classed as no

Left : **Holland's Johan Neeskens (orange shirt) faces Telch of Argentina in a 1974 World Cup match between the two countries which Holland won 4–0. A club-mate of Johan Cruyff's at both Ajax and Barcelona, Neeskens is now with New York Cosmos.**

Above : **A superbly skilled right-sided midfield player, Italy's Franco Causio (left), has often been Romeo Benetti's midfield foil in the Italian national side. Here, he takes the ball past French defender Maxime Bossis during a 1978 game which Italy won 2–1.**

more than basically competent in midfield, although in Yorath of Tottenham, Wales have a good, if ageing, ball-winner and in McCreery of Queens Park Rangers and McIlroy of Manchester United, two players good in both midfield and attack, Northern Ireland do at least have some hope for the future.

But the most highly skilled young midfield player in Britain today is ineligible to play for any of these teams. His name is Liam Brady, he is an Eire international and he plays his League soccer for Arsenal. For one so young—he's in his early twenties—Brady is a player of remarkable maturity and skill. His display for Arsenal in the 1979 FA Cup Final against Manchester United was a true match-winning performance as he totally dominated midfield and had a hand in each of Arsenal's goals in their 3-2 win. His only real weakness at present would seem to be a susceptibility to lose effectiveness when subjected to tight marking—although trying to stick with a player of Brady's mercurial skills is never the easiest of tasks. However, as he learns more and more how to 'lose' a marker, Brady's midfield effectiveness can only increase. It is regrettable that playing for Eire—a vastly improved but still patchy international side—Brady is unlikely ever to appear in the final stages of the World Cup and so be given the opportunity to display his enormous talents in front of a wider audience than at present.

The only player in Europe currently on a par with Brady in terms of age and achievement is Michel Platini of France, who also has the combined skills of both goal-scorer and goal-maker. But whereas Brady's interest in the World Cup ended with Eire's elimination by, coincidentally, France, Platini had a tremendous tournament and although his team had the misfortune to be drawn in the strongest first round group along with Italy, Argentina and Hungary, a draw that effectively ended their chances, Platini showed that he can survive and prosper in the very best of company. Brady still patiently waits for the chance to do likewise.

Previous page: **A personal duel between Kenny Dalglish (red shirt) and John Wile (stripes), demonstrates the pressures to which the top grade players are subjected. To stop Dalglish, Wile commits a 'professional' foul, a non-injurious tug at Dalglish's shirt on the referee's blind side—illegal in every respect, but near-impossible to stamp out.**

Right above: **The power and presence of Romeo Benetti in midfield for Italy was often a daunting prospect for opponents during the latter half of the Seventies. Extremely skilful for a man of his size, Benetti's many subtleties during a game would belie his 'hard man' image. He is one of the author's midfield selections for the 'World's Best Team' later in the book.**

Right: **Two of Britain's best midfield players, Tony Currie (white shirt) and Graeme Souness contest for the ball during this England v Scotland game. In the background, England's Trevor Brooking awaits the outcome of their tussle. Currie had the last laugh in this instance—England won 3–1.**

Far right: **Sheer determination and will to win are the over-riding emotions on the face of Holland's Arie Haan (orange shirt), as he brushes aside a challenge from Argentina's Jorge Olguin. Haan has had a glittering career at club and international level, appearing in two World Cup Finals and three winning European Cup teams.**

3

The Defenders

Systems and players in today's game

From forwards, goalkeepers and midfielders, the spotlight now turns on to defenders, for irrespective of whether a team plays 4-2-4, 4-3-3 or 4-4-2, one factor remains constant—despite the re-arrangement of numbers in midfield or attack, the norm in all these formations makes provision for four defensive players.

Generally speaking, all back fours comprise two full backs, whose prime task it is to cover the wings, and a centre-half to 'bottle up' the middle. The fourth defender is generally used in one of three ways: as a 'twin' centre-half; as a sweeper, playing slightly in front of, or slightly behind, the main defensive formation; or else as a player with special marking responsibilities. Of course, there are national variations to these formats, most notably in Italy, where a fifth

defender operates behind the back four as a lateral sweeper, giving a 1-4-3-2 formation. This particular line-up is known as the *catenaccio* or 'bolt' and is largely responsible for the negative, defensive soccer that bedevils the Italian game, where the rewards for winning are so great that the chief motivating factor among clubs at the top level has become to avoid defeat at all costs.

Elsewhere on the Continent, the accent is largely on man-to-man marking. In other words, each member of the back four is given the job of marking a specific opponent, in contrast to the system favoured in British soccer, which involves a defender 'marking space'. In this instance, each defender will be given a specific area—as opposed to a specific player—to mark and his task then is to pick up any opposing player who comes within his own particular area. This tactic is known as the 'zonal defence system' and it perhaps has advantages over man-to-man marking, making it more difficult for a skilful forward to pull a defender out of position

Previous page: **Scotland's Joe Jordan (no 9, blue shirt) loses out with this aerial challenge to England's Dave Watson during this British International Championship game at Wembley in May 1979 which England won 3–1. Also in Scotland's team are Arthur Graham (no 11), Graeme Souness and Gordon McQueen.**

Below: **High jinks as Italy's Marco Tardelli (no 14) and France's centre-forward Bernard Lacombe go for a high ball. Earlier in this 1978 World Cup game, Lacombe had scored the first and fastest goal of the Tournament, netting after less than a minute's play, but Italy still went on to win 2–1.**

Although being a defender is a less glamorous job than making or scoring goals, two of the greatest players to grace soccer in modern times both made their reputations as defensive players. The first was Bobby Moore, who captained England in 1966. Moore was perhaps the finest defensive half-back ever to play for England; a shrewd tactician and a fine reader of the game, he was totally unflappable under pressure. His calm reassurance in defence, added to his ability to set up attacks from deep in his own half, was rewarded by a record 108 appearances for England.

Fine player though Moore was, however, even he would concede that in the modern era the greatest defensive player of all was West Germany's Franz Beckenbauer, who appeared 103 times for his country and led them to victory in the 1974 World Cup. Beckenbauer's style of play innovated a completely new tactical formation, both with his club Bayern Munich (winners of the European Cup in three consecutive years from 1974) and with West Germany. Known as the *libero*, the tactic involved Beckenbauer playing as a 'forward sweeper' ahead of the main defensive formation, but behind the midfield players—in effect, a 3-1-3-3. In this way, Beckenbauer was both the first line of defence and the springboard for attacks. Because of the scope of his role, Beckenbauer was almost impossible to mark. One moment might see him defending in his own penalty area; the next he would be embarking on a long surging run upfield, or unleashing a pinpoint accurate pass of some 30 or 40 yards (30 or 40 metres) to set up an attack from the very depths of defence. Unlike Moore, who only scored twice in his entire international career, Beckenbauer scored a number of goals for both club and country, most notably during the 1966 World Cup finals when, playing in a midfield role he scored four in six games.

Part of the reason for Beckenbauer's effectiveness was the extreme capability of his co-defenders. For long periods during the 1970s, West Germany's back four were automatic choices, with Berti Vogts, George Schwarzenbeck and Paul Breitner making up the numbers. Vogts was a terrier-like player, excelling in man-to-man marking; Schwarzenbeck, although not really a man in the traditional centre-half mould, was nevertheless an effective central defender; while Breitner was a brilliant attacking full-back, unafraid to lend support to midfield, but fast and sure in his recovery back into defence. Further effectiveness came from the fact that as Beckenbauer, Schwarzenbeck and Breitner all played for Bayern Munich, they each knew the others' style of play to perfection and so dovetailed into a vastly experienced unit. For all their skills, however, the team's defensive orchestrator was Beckenbauer —Kaiser Franz, as he came to be known—who controlled his players to perfection, bringing out the best from each and giving new depth to the role of soccer team captain.

If Moore and Beckenbauer represent the height of defensive play from an overall viewpoint, then in specialist

Right: **Unquestionably *the* defensive player of his generation, West Germany's Franz Beckenbauer guided both his country and his club Bayern Munich to the top honours that world soccer has to offer. Now in the twilight of his outstanding career, Beckenbauer is in his third season with the NASL club New York Cosmos.**

positions, several players in the game today are also of true world class. In the 1978 World Cup Final, the two opposing central defenders represented perhaps the world's best. Argentina's Daniel Passarella and Holland's Rudi Krol both had inspired tournaments, with Passarella in particular captaining his side perfectly, keeping a tight rein on some of his colleagues' wilder tendencies and marshalling his defence as a tight and effective unit. Krol—although not an orthodox centre-half in the strictest sense of the word, as a disciple of the Dutch school of 'total football'—was a more adventurous player, equally at home in the opposing penalty area as his own, but for all that, no less effective as a defender.

At present, Krol has few peers in European soccer, where for some reason there is a current dearth of good centre-halves. From Britain, Dave Watson of England—the incumbent during 1979 and early 1980—is now well into the veteran stage. After leaving Manchester City to play out the remainder of his career with the German *Bundesligia* (First Division) side Werder Bremen, he found that he and continental soccer weren't the best of companions. Sent off for hitting an opponent in an early game, he never really settled and returned to England with Southampton, where's he's teamed up with Kevin Keegan. Scotland are at present experimenting with the centre-half position, while Wales have never found a really adequate replacement for Mike England, who left League soccer for America where, with Seattle Sounders, in each year from 1975 to 1978 inclusive, he was voted into the prestigious NASL 'All Star

Left: **A familiar sight in Argentina's team during 1978 was the afro hair-style of Alberto Tarantini. He is pictured here playing for the English club Birmingham City, who signed him for the 1978/9 Football League season. But Tarantini was unable to recapture his World Cup form or to settle in England and returned to his native Argentina after only one season. He was one of several unfortunate internationals who found moving to England was detrimental.**

Below: **Argentina's Daniel Passarella (striped shirt), was perhaps the 1978 World Cup's outstanding central defender. His captaincy was an inspiration to his side and his fearless play is illustrated by this diving header to clear the ball away from Holland's Dick Nanninga during the Final. It was a final of quite astonishing emotion. The Argentinian crowd was nearly hysterical anticipating a win for their national team which would have made them the premier footballing nation in the world.**

Above: England's World Cup-winning captain in 1966 and the holder of a record 108 international caps for his country, Bobby Moore was one of soccer's most influential defensive players. On leaving English League soccer, Moore had short spells with San Antonio and Seattle in the NASL before returning to England to enter club management.

Right above: The mind of Brazil's Nelinho (no 14) seems anywhere but on the apparent challenge of Scotland's Archie Gemmill.

Scotland have never beaten the three-time World Champions and indeed have only scored against them once.

Far right: **Captain meets captain. West Germany's Berti Vogts (white shirt), approaches his Austrian opposite number Robert Sara. One of the most tireless defensive workers and most effective close-markers in the game, Vogts took over the West German captaincy from Franz Beckenbauer, but was unable to guide his country to a successful defence of the World Cup they won in 1974.**

Team', a selection made by players, coaches and American soccer writers. Northern Ireland still rely on the veteran Alan Hunter of Ipswich.

But while Britain bemoans the lack of good centre-halves, Eire—already blessed with Liam Brady—are in the happy position of having two of the finest young prospects in all Europe playing for their international side—David O'Leary of Arsenal and Brighton's Mark Lawrenson. The latter has almost limitless promise and with a little more top-flight experience will become a player of immense stature.

As for the rest in Europe, the pick of the crop is probably France's 1978 World Cup captain Marius Tresor who plays for Marseille in the French First Division. Because of France's early elimination from the tournament's final stages, Tresor was given scant opportunity to show his undoubted skills both as a player and as an international captain.

If there is a current dearth of good central defenders, either already established or whose best days are yet to come, the situation as regards full-backs—in England at any rate—is by comparison rich with promise. English soccer has something of a tradition in turning out fine players in this particular position, from Male and Hapgood, the celebrated Arsenal and England backs of the 1930s, via Alf Ramsey during his career as a player with Southampton and Tottenham in the 1950s to George Cohen and Ray Wilson, the full-backs in England's 1966 World Cup team. Utilizing a 4-3-3 formation, that particular side was christened 'the wingless wonders', but Cohen and Wilson—right and left backs respectively—made up for the lack of orthodox wingers by adopting the role themselves, breaking on the overlap and setting a precedent for full-back play that has remained a constant factor in the game ever since.

At present, England is fortunate in having three of the brightest young full-back prospects in the game in Viv Anderson of Nottingham Forest (the first black player ever to represent England at full international level), Kenny Sansom of Crystal Palace (another full international) and West Bromwich Albion's Derek Statham. These players—and indeed most like them in the British game at present—fully realize the responsibilities of the 'new' art of full-back play. Until 1966, the duties of the full-back were purely defensive. Opposed by wingers, speed was perhaps the defensive full-back's most important attribute, closely followed by his skill in the tackle. With experience, a full-back could tell whether a winger would attempt to go outside him by taking the ball along the touchline and down to the goal-line before crossing, or alternatively cut inside heading on a diagonal run towards goal.

The majority of all wingers favoured just one of these two approaches. A left-footed player on the left wing would be more likely to keep the ball on his stronger foot by going outside the back, and the same applied to a right-footed

player on the right wing. Conversely, a right-footed player on the left wing would be more likely to keep the ball on his stronger foot by cutting inside—as would a left-footed player on the right-hand side of the field—so the art of good full-back play involved trying to make the winger play the ball on his weaker foot and thus reduce his effectiveness.

For example, if a back was facing a naturally left-footed winger on the left-hand side of the field, he knew that for all the winger's feints and trickery, he would be trying to keep the ball on his stronger foot. The back would therefore try to shepherd the winger inside, forcing the ball on to his weaker foot until the right moment to put in the tackle. The winger for his part would use every trick in the book to wrong-foot the back. If he actually *wanted* to hug the touchline, he would feint to cut *inside*, drawing the back off-balance before kicking the ball past him on the *outside* and darting past before the back had recovered his balance.

The greatest master of this art was the legendary Stanley Matthews, a right-footed, right winger who preferred—naturally enough—to take the ball on to his stronger right foot and go down the touchline before crossing. With English League soccer being the close-knit sort of game it is, not a full-back in the land was unaware of the Matthews technique, yet most struggled when faced with marking him. Why? Time and again, Matthews would shuffle up to the back who *knew* through experience, through coaching and through common sense that whatever Matthews might feint to do, he would in fact ultimately take the ball on to his right foot. So he would watch Matthews sway over to the left, unconsciously almost

following his movement. The sway would become more pronounced until it seemed that this was the one time the norm wasn't going to apply. Accordingly, he would shift his weight and balance and in that split-instant, Matthews would drag the ball back on to his right foot, flicking it past the now hopelessly off-balance back with the delicacy and precision of a surgeon's scalpel. Time after time coaches tried to drum into a player whose thankless task it was to mark Matthews that the right foot was the danger. Time after time their words proved fruitless.

With the demise of wingers in the Matthews tradition and the advent of 4-3-3, the art of full-back play changed. Left now without a specific man to mark and to make up for the absence of wingers in their own side, backs in the British game were encouraged by managers and coaches to add an attacking dimension to their play. If Cohen and Wilson were the first exponents of this technique, the tradition has remained ever since and it is now the exception rather than the norm for a team to include an out-and-out defensive back with no attacking responsibilities whatsoever, although this factor does not hold quite as strongly on the Continent, where the basic necessities of man-to-man marking do to an extent preclude the back from venturing too far upfield.

This being the case, there are still some outstanding examples of purely defensive backs playing in European soccer. Italy in particular, with its heavy accent on defence, seems to produce an almost endless supply of such players, not least of whom were the full-back pairing of Scirea and Cabrini during 1978. West Germany's Berti Vogts, perhaps

the best defensive full-back in the world, retired at the end of the 1979 season in the best possible manner, captaining his side Borussia Moenchengladbach to victory over Red Star Belgrade to win the UEFA Cup—the second time in five years that Borussia had finished winners of the trophy.

But the European game does not only produce defensive full-backs. A vital member of the Dutch defence in both the 1974 and 1978 World Cups alongside Rudi Krol was Wim Suurbier and another who also made the trip from Munich to Buenos Aires was Wim Rijsbergen. Although ostensibly defenders, both Suurbier and Rijsbergen, in common with the rest of the Dutch side very much immersed in the 'total football' philosophy, were familiar sights raiding down the wings in both World Cup tournaments.

From South America, three full-backs made their mark during the 1978 World Cup. Most notable by his sheer physical presence was Argentina's afro-haired Alberto Tarantini, who scored one of his country's vital goals against Peru. Such was the impact made by Tarantini during the tournament that he joined Argentina's two other expensive exports Osavaldo Ardiles and Ricardo Villa in English League soccer during the following season. Sadly, though Ardiles had a magnificent debut season and Villa a promising one with Tottenham, Tarantini found himself plunged into the midst of a losing battle against relegation with Birmingham City, never really settled for both professional and personal reasons, and departed for home at the end of his first season, perhaps not unhappy to swap the Midlands for more familiar surroundings. In addition to Tarantini, the other backs to

catch the eye during 1978 were the Brazilian pair of Nelinho and Toninho, the former in particular a player of real class, carrying on where the likes of Nilton and Djalma Santos and Francisco Marinho left off.

For the future, it's difficult to see how the general role of defenders will develop, bearing in mind that in the space of less than a decade players in these positions have become far more skilled in ball-playing terms than their predecessors, and in many cases are now regular and important goal-scorers for their sides. It's quite likely that the offensive role of full-backs will be developed still further than at present, where the overlap down the wing currently marks the limit of forward involvement. Perhaps a slight push forward into the midfield areas—congesting this already busy section still further—might be the next step. As for centre-halves, how ironic it would be if their role were to revert full-circle to the days of over 50 years ago when the position was an attacking one. Although the confines and patterns of the modern game would make this difficult, it's not unknown today for a side to play without a recognised 'stopper'— a pointer maybe to the future.

Left: **England's Phil Neale winces as a perfectly delivered right hook from Scotland's Joe Jordan catches him in the throat. Arthur Graham, oblivious to the fisticuffs, seems more intent on chasing the ball and getting on with the game.**

Below: **After an outstanding career with Ajax Amsterdam and Holland, Wim Suurbier (no 19) has now joined his former team-mate and captain Johan Cruyff with Los Angeles Aztecs, for whom he is playing here against Washington Diplomats.**

International Soccer

The World Cup and European Championships

In the field of international soccer, one tournament stands head and shoulders above all others. The FIFA (Federation of International Football Associations) World Cup, to give the competition its full title, is perhaps the most prestigious trophy in all professional sport and the finals, which are held every four years, attract a world-wide television audience of staggering proportions.

Originally known as the Jules Rimet Cup (in honour of the first President of FIFA), the trophy was first competed for in 1930 when Uruguay was the host nation. A mere 13 countries entered teams for that first competition—a stark contrast to the 100-plus entries for the 1978 tournament— and it was duly won by Uruguay, who defeated Argentina 4-2 in the Final. Since 1930, there have been 10 World Cups, but just six nations have won the coveted trophy: Brazil (in 1958, 1962 and 1970, the last win giving them the outright possession of the Jules Rimet Cup and necessitating the appearance of a second trophy); Uruguay (in 1930 and 1950); Italy (in 1934 and 1938); West Germany (in 1954 and 1974); England (in 1966); and Argentina (in 1978). Additionally, eight countries have supplied losing finalists: Czechoslovakia (in 1934 and 1962); Hungary (in 1938 and 1954); Holland (in 1974 and 1978); Argentina (in 1930); Brazil (in 1950); West Germany (in 1966); Italy (in 1970); and Sweden (in 1958). Clearly Brazil's record of four appearances in 11 Finals is unparalleled, although closely pressed by the three Final appearances of both Italy and West Germany. But the country to which one's heart goes out is Holland who in the two most recent competitions have suffered the morale-shattering experience of reaching the Final only to lose to the host nation.

In 1974, West Germany, then the current European champions, played host to the world and started as one of the four favourites—the others were Holland, Brazil and Italy. The Italians were grouped with Argentina, Poland (the conquerors of England during the tournament's early qualifying stages), and Haiti. The opening match for the Italians against Haiti provided an early unsettling moment as the underdogs actually managed to score first, but the Italians kept their heads and finished 3-1 winners. Next came Argentina who had already lost 3-2 to Poland, but who held Italy to a 1-1 draw. Poland meanwhile were annihilating Haiti 7-0 to make sure of their place in the competition's next stage, so the Italians came face to face with the prospect of having to actually beat Poland to go through to the next round ahead of Argentina. As it was, the game ended in cataclysmic 2-1 defeat for the Italians, who were then further rocked by allegations (never proved) from the Polish camp that during the match itself, Italian players had attempted to bribe their Polish counterparts into throwing the game.

So Poland, the surprise package of the tournament, came through to one of the two final qualifying groups. So did Brazil, then the current World Cup holders; in retrospect perhaps too much was expected of them, bearing in mind that Pele, Gerson, Tostao and Clodoaldo from the winning team of 1970 were all missing. However, in Leao they had one of the finest goalkeepers of the tournament; the big, blond left-back Francisco Marinho was a tower of strength in defence, while the left-foot power of Rivelino was responsible for some truly stunning goals. Grouped with Yugoslavia, Scotland and Zaire, Brazil's early performances were unimpressive. A goalless draw against Yugoslavia was followed by a similar scoreline against Scotland, which left Brazil facing Zaire in their final game needing to win by at least three clear goals to qualify for the final stages on goal difference ahead of Scotland. They achieved the bare minimum—a 3-0 win, the crucial goal being a sloppy effort which in any other game the Zaire goalkeeper would probably have prevented. So Brazil went through to the last eight along with Yugoslavia while Scotland, undefeated in all games but paying for their lack of scoring power, returned home reflecting on their misfortune at being eliminated from the tournament on goal difference alone.

Holland's progress to the last eight was, with one slight hiccup, serene. Drawn with Sweden, Bulgaria and Uruguay,

they opened with a 2-0 win over the latter in an ugly game during which the Uruguayans seemed intent on maiming anyone wearing an orange shirt. In the end, Castillo, by no means the worst offender, was sent off for hitting Rensenbrink. Holland's next game—against Sweden—provided the hiccup in the shape of a 0-0 draw, with Ronnie Hellstroem in the Swedish goal producing heroics and even the wiles of Johan Cruyff subdued by a tight and well-marshalled defence. A 4-1 win over Bulgaria, helped by a couple of penalties, ensured Holland's passage to the World Cup's next stage, while Sweden beat a demoralized Uruguay 3-0 to join them.

West Germany were grouped with Chile, Australia and East Germany, hardly the most demanding of oppositions, yet made uncharacteristically heavy weather of those three games. An unimpressive 1-0 win over Chile was followed by an easy 3-0 victory over Australia before East Germany—who had beaten Australia and drawn with Chile—upset the nationalistic applecart with a 1-0 win. That game with East Germany was a strange one. West Germany, by virtue of their wins over Australia and Chile, had already ensured their place in the last eight and although East Germany had a mathematical chance of being overtaken by Chile, they too seemed assured of going forward. Their 1-0 win over their greatest rivals was of course a fine achievement, although the resulting celebrations were tempered by the knowledge that their next series of games would be against Holland, Brazil and Argentina, whereas West Germany's opponents were Poland, Sweden and Yugoslavia.

At the time of this West German defeat, views were expressed—with more than a trace of cynicism—that the side was somewhat less than heartbroken at losing, for had they beaten East Germany, *they* would have gone in with Holland, Brazil and Argentina—a far tougher prospect than the countries they were now actually to meet.

As it turned out, the cynics were perhaps proved right. West Germany opened with a comfortable 2-0 win over Yugoslavia—the weakest of the group's teams—and beat Sweden 4-2 in a wonderful game before coming up against Poland. For their part, the Poles had slightly closer 1-0 and 2-1 wins over Sweden (who missed a penalty) and Yugoslavia respectively. The game with West Germany was now effectively a semi-final, with the winner going into the World Cup Final itself, so the match, played in Frankfurt, was obviously of huge importance to both. The game was played under appalling water-logged conditions and was settled by a single goal scored in the second half by the irrepressible Gerd Muller, after his side had earlier shown astonishing profligacy in missing a penalty.

If West Germany's passage to the 1974 World Cup Final was eventually slightly fraught, Holland's was simply majestic. First Argentina were hammered 4-0 with Cruyff scoring twice. Then East Germany's interest in the competition ended with a 2-0 defeat. The third game against Brazil also assumed the semi-final proportions of West Germany versus Poland, for Brazil had also beaten Argentina and East Germany, and although Holland (and West Germany too) would have both qualified for the Final on goal difference in the event of a draw, neither could afford to lose such an important match.

Left above: **The surprise packet of the 1978 World Cup finals was Tunisia, seen here in a qualifying game against red-shirted Egypt which they won 4–1 to make sure of reaching Argentina, where they achieved the distinction of holding mighty West Germany to a 0–0 draw in addition to beating Mexico 3–1.**

Right above: **The Italian wall breaks to block a free-kick by Perfumo during this 1974 Group 4 World Cup match. Although denied on** this particular occasion, Perfumo eventually did get his name on the score-sheet—by putting through his own goal to give Italy a 1–1 draw.

Above: **The Brazil v Spain Group 3 World Cup game played at Mar del Plata during the 1978 Tournament was chiefly notable for its tedium brought on by the defensive stranglehold both sides imposed on the game. Scoring chances like this were few and the result was a 0–0 draw.**

Cruyff—with a sensational flying volley that was perhaps the goal of the tournament in both build-up and execution—notched the second to send Holland into the Final against West Germany while Brazil were left to meet Poland in the match for third place which the Poles—justly perhaps in view of their sterling performances right from the very start of the competition—won 1-0.

The Final itself, played in Munich's Olympic Stadium on July 7, 1974, was a disappointing affair, although on paper it was a dream game with Holland's Cruyff-inspired 'total football' versus West Germany's Beckenbauer-dominated *libero* system. Within a minute, Holland were a goal up. Hoeness fouled Cruyff in the box and Neeskens banged home the resulting penalty. When West Germany kicked off to restart, it was the first time any of their players had touched the ball. A lesser side might have crumbled, but the Germans stuck to their task with Vogts striving manfully to subdue Cruyff (and eventually succeeding) and Beckenbauer stamping his tempo on the game. Midway through the first half West Germany equalized from a Breitner penalty after Holzenbein had been fouled in the area, and just before half-time, they scored what was to prove the winning goal when Gerd Muller scored from close range after the Dutch defence had only half-cleared an attack.

So West Germany became world champions, but who would have guessed at the moment Franz Beckenbauer held the trophy aloft in victory that four years later West Germany would be sunk almost without trace while Holland were stepping out to contest their second successive Final?

In 1978, England again failed to qualify—this time pipped on goal difference by Italy—and it was again left to Scotland to carry Britain's hopes. West Germany, as holders, automatically qualified to defend their title. So did Argentina as host nation. Holland, without Cruyff but with the majority of the 1974 side still there, were back, as were Poland and Sweden. From South America, along with Argentina, Brazil and Peru were there.

The pre-tournament favourites were Argentina (more on the precedent of previous host nation wins rather than in admiration of their side), Holland, West Germany, Italy and, with hideous optimism as events were to prove, Scotland. The first of the four preliminary qualifying groups, and by some way the toughest, contained Italy, Argentina, France and Hungary. Both Italy and Argentina had wins over France and Hungary to ensure their passage to the last eight before themselves meeting in Buenos Aires. Traumatically, Argentina went down 1-0 although, as events later showed, this defeat paradoxically was to slightly ease their path to the Final because Italy's second series matches were far harder, while Argentina, with one exception, found theirs were less demanding.

Poland and West Germany found themselves paired with seemingly easy opposition in the shape of Tunisia and Mexico. But, though both duly qualified for the last eight, their passage was shaken by two almighty shocks from the

Although the Brazilians had gained in confidence throughout the competition and reached the Holland game playing something that approached a recognizable form of 'Brazilian soccer', they seemed undecided as to whether to attempt to play the Dutch off the pitch or kick them off. Not that Holland were a bunch of shrinking violets, and some of the fouls committed by both sets of players curdled the blood —in particular, Mario Marinho's flattening of Johan Neeskens (which the referee claimed not to have seen) and Pereira's foul on the same player (which the referee could hardly have avoided seeing, such was its blatancy) which led to the Brazilian being sent off. In spite of, or maybe because of, the flying boots, Holland won the day. Neeskens, who had something of an unforgettable match, scored the first and

Next page: **England centre-forward Bob Latchford sweeps the ball past Czech goalkeeper Michalik during a** **friendly game between the two countries played at Wembley in November 1978. England won 1–0.**

Top: **Austrian striker Hans Krankl gets the better of this particular tackle from Brazil's outstanding defender Toninho during the 1978 Group 3 World Cup match between the two countries which Brazil won 1-0. Krankl had a particularly good tournament and his form continued in the Spanish League with Barcelona the next season.**

Above: **Despite being grounded and receiving the close attention of Yugoslavia's Buljan (left) and Katalinski (right), West Germany's Gerd Muller still managed to score his country's second goal of a 2–0 win in this 1974 World Cup game. Now, American audiences are treated to Muller's goal-scoring skills with Tampa Bay Rowdies in the NASL.**

right awaited them and slunk off 90 minutes later at the wrong end of a 3-1 scoreline. Scottish demoralization was completed when a post-match dope test on their winger Willie Johnstone proved positive, thereby ensuring his early exit from the tournament. Scotland's next game was a feeble 1-1 draw with Iran, yet they came to their final match against Holland with a chance of qualifying for the last eight. This was due to the fact that Holland, although victors over Iran, had only drawn with Peru. With Peru already through to the last eight, if Scotland were to have won their game against Holland by three clear goals, they and not the beaten 1974 finalists would have gone forward on goal difference. Rising to the challenge, the Scots, with typical national perversity, played their game of the tournament and at one stage were 3-1 ahead, just one tantalizing goal away from glory, before Holland's Johnny Rep scored the goal to ensure that his country, despite defeat, would go forward on goal difference.

Unlike 1974, there were no 'easy' games in the final two groups: Holland, Italy, West Germany and Austria in one; Argentina, Brazil, Poland and Peru in the other. After the Germans and the Italians had played out a sterile 0-0 draw, Holland ran glorious riot over Austria, winning 5-1. Italy then beat Austria, too, though only 1-0, before Holland and West Germany met in a repeat of the 1974 Final. For the Dutch, there was no Cruyff and no Van Hanegem, although Haan, Neeskens, Rep, Krol, Jansen, Rensenbrink and Rene van der Kerkhof had all appeared in the 1974 Final. West Germany were more seriously decimated, with Beckenbauer, Muller, Schwarzenbeck, Breitner, Hoeness, Overath and Grabowski all absent from Munich. Against the odds, Germany built up a 2-1 lead and held it until just seven minutes from time, when Rene van der Kerkhof scored the equalizer. Holland then effectively ended Italy's chances with a fine 2-1 win which qualified them for the Final and made West Germany's last game against Austria of mere academic interest. That the Austrians had a memorable 3-2 win only underlined West Germany's decline.

The second group turned into a straight fight between Argentina and Brazil. The two drew with each other and then Brazil recorded wins over Poland (as did Argentina) and Peru. That left Argentina facing Peru with the stiff task of winning by at least four clear goals to qualify for the Final ahead of Brazil on goal difference. Somewhat improbably, they did just that, winning 6-0 in a game during which their twin spearheads of Kempes and Luque each scored twice to leave Brazil muttering darkly about the eccentricities of Peru's goalie Ramon Quiroga, who by a quirk of fate just happened to have been born in Argentina. For their part, Brazil—the only team to come through the final stages of the tournament unbeaten—gained some reward with a 2-1 win over Italy in the play-off for third place.

So to the Final between Argentina and Holland. As in past games of this importance, the pressures told on both sets of players and although the games was undeniably exciting, for the most part the skill factor was largely missing. Kempes gave his country the lead late in the first half and the score remained 1-0 until just eight minutes from time when Nanninga, substituting for Rep, equalized. A Rensenbrink effort that would have given Holland victory shaved an upright

unheralded Tunisians who, playing a delightfully exuberant and direct game, were first desperately unlucky to lose 1-0 to Poland before surpassing themselves with a 0-0 draw against the mighty West Germans. The Mexicans were beaten out of sight by everyone, most notably by West Germany who put six goals past them without reply—a win that flattered to deceive.

The third group saw Brazil teamed with Austria, Spain and Sweden. Sweden were not the canny outfit of four years earlier, while Spain—perhaps with half an eye on 1982 when they are due to host the finals—found a draw with Brazil and a win over Sweden not quite enough to send them into the last eight. In addition to drawing with Spain, Brazil also drew with Sweden before beating Austria to go into the tournament's next round, while the Austrians found that wins over both Spain and Sweden was enough to accompany Brazil.

In Group 4, comprising Scotland, Holland, Peru and Iran, Scotland strode out against Peru as if victory by divine

Above: **Bjorn Nordqvist (no 4) and Ralf Edstrom can't stop the green-shirted Gerd Muller from getting in a shot during this 1974 World Cup** **game. After a magnificent contest, West Germany finished 4–2 winners, but surprisingly Muller was not among the scorers.**

Svehlik and Dobias to one from Dieter Muller (no relation to in the very last minute, but with the score tied at 1-1, the game went into extra time. Urged on by their marvellously-behaved fans, Argentina took the lead, through Kempes again in the first extra time period, and then in the second Bertoni put the issue beyond doubt to make the final score 3-1. Though victory was Argentina's, the sympathy lay with Holland and only time will tell whether they have recovered from that second shattering World Cup Final defeat.

On a lesser scale to the World Cup, though no less fiercely contested, is the European Championship (formerly known as the European Nations Cup) which was first competed for in 1960. Played in the two years after each World Cup finals, the winners have been Russia (in 1960); Spain (in 1964); Italy (in 1968); West Germany (in 1972); and Czechoslovakia (in 1976). The last competition, the final stages of which were held in Yugoslavia, was an extraordinary affair in which the underdogs had the last laugh at almost every stage. Holland, West Germany and Czechoslovakia, together with the host nation, won through to the semi-finals and when Holland and West Germany managed to avoid each other in the draw, the stage seemed set for a repeat of the 1974 World Cup Final. But Holland's opponents Czechoslovakia had other ideas, winning the game 3-1 after extra time despite the fact that Holland had seven of their World Cup Final team playing. Yugoslavia gave West Germany a fright too, before the world champions won 4-2 in another extra time game. The Final, played between West Germany and Czechoslovakia, turned into yet another extra-time affair. Goals from

the celebrated Gerd) had the Czechs 2-1 up at half-time and they held that lead until the very last minute of play when Holzenbein popped in the equalizer. Extra time came and went without any addition to the score, so it was left for the championship to be decided (thoroughly unsatisfactorily) on penalties. The Czechs scored with each of their five attempts; the West Germans managed only three so, improbably, the reigning world champions were beaten. That the Czechs were basically no more than a good side having a great run was amply demonstrated by their easy elimination from the primary qualifying stages of the 1978 World Cup by—of all teams—Scotland.

Ranking alongside the European Championship *should* be its South American equivalent the America Cup (formerly the South American Championship). 'Should' because in practice, far more weight is given to the inter-club competition the Copa Libertadores. In the past, championship entries have not been fully-representative national sides (which has led to a falling-off of spectator interest) while tournaments have tended to be held on an irregular basis. Peru are the current official South American champions by virtue of their victory in the South American Championship in 1975. Hopefully, the new America Cup which was inaugurated in 1979 will prove a more viable and popular successor.

5

Cups and Clubs

International club competitions

If the World Cup is soccer's premier competition for international sides, the club equivalent would logically seem to be the World Club Championship, but for reasons that will be explained later in this chapter, this just isn't so. Depending on whether you are a South American or a European, your loyalties and interest will be captured by the Copa Libertadores and the European Cup respectively, together with the latter's two sister competitions the European Cup-Winners Cup and the UEFA (Union of European Football Associations) Cup, and, to a far smaller extent, the so-called European Super Cup.

The oldest of these international club competitions is the European Cup (or to give the competition its full title, the European Champions Cup) which was inaugurated in the 1955/6 season. Entry is restricted to the current Division 1 champions of each European nation, plus the previous year's winners. With the exception of the Final, ties are decided on a two-game, home-and-away basis and the winners are the side with the higher aggregate score. To avoid the need for time-consuming play-offs should these aggregate scores finish level after two games, away goals count 'double' in the event of a tie—a crude but reasonably effective way of settling the issue. So, for example, if team A loses 3-1 away to team B, but wins the return 2-0, team A goes through on the away goals rule. If both games should finish 3-1,

extra time is played and if the deadlock is still unbroken, penalty kicks decide the outcome.

The first five years of the European Cup were dominated by one side, Real Madrid, who won the trophy from 1956-1960 inclusive and marked the end of their run with a sensational 7-3 win over Eintracht Frankfurt before 136,000 spectators at Hampden Park in Glasgow. The European Cup stayed in the Iberian Peninsular for the next two years with the Portuguese club Benfica, before going to Italy three years running with wins for AC Milan and Inter-Milan (twice). In 1966, Real Madrid were champions again before Glasgow Celtic became the first ever British side to win the trophy with a 2-1 win over Inter-Milan in Lisbon.

The following year, Manchester United marked the tenth anniversary of the Munich Air Disaster by bringing the trophy to England for the first time with a heart-stopping 4-1 extra time win over Benfica at Wembley. AC Milan were winners again in 1969, but this was to be the last time a southern European side emerged as victors for the next decade; ever since, the European Cup has been dominated by three countries—Holland, West Germany and England.

Feyenoord of Rotterdam began this northern supremacy in 1970 before the Johan Cruyff-inspired Ajax Amsterdam took the trophy three years running. In 1974, the spotlight switched to West Germany where Bayern Munich—including Franz Beckenbauer, Gerd Muller and several others from West Germany's World Cup-winning side—recorded the first of their three successive wins. In 1977, the Cup returned to England with Liverpool, for whom victory was the logical succession to five years of total supremacy in the domestic game with three First Division titles (and two runners-up placings) and an FA Cup win. Abroad, too, they had shown their power with UEFA Cup wins in 1973 and 1976. Until 1977, however, the big one had always eluded them.

Liverpool began their Cup-winning run easily enough with a 7-0 aggregate win over the Irish side Crusaders. Next came the Turkish champions Trabzonspor who provided slightly sterner opposition by winning their home leg 1-0 before going down 3-0 in Liverpool. In the quarter-finals, Liverpool were drawn with the excellent side French St Etienne, who had lost by just 1-0 to Bayern Munich in the previous year's Final. Although St Etienne won 1-0 in France, they too were ousted at Anfield, losing 3-1. Apart from Liverpool, the other three sides to reach the semi-finals were

Previous page: In 1977, Nottingham Forest were in the Second Division of the English Football League. In 1979, revitalized by the charismatic managerial skills of Brian Clough, they won the European Cup—surely one of the most dramatic rises to prominence from obscurity.

Left: **Arsenal's 3–2 win over Manchester Utd in the 1979 Cup Final was one of the most dramatic of recent years. Here, Alan Sunderland (yellow shirt, arms raised) and Brian Talbot (yellow shirt, legs in air), have both just bundled the ball into the net to give Arsenal a 1–0 lead.**

Right above: **Bayern Munich goalie Sepp Maier makes a flying catch to gather the ball from the white-shirted Alan Clarke of Leeds Utd during the 1975 European Cup Final in Paris. Bayern won a rather** sour match 2–0, the second of their three successive European Cup wins in the Seventies.

Right: **Having turned in a brilliant display to win the European Cup in 1977, Liverpool retained the trophy in 1978, winning a dull, dour and ultimately disappointing Final against FC Bruges by 1–0 at Wembley. Seven white-shirted Belgian players can be seen in or around their own penalty area—a measure of their stultifying tactics during this game.**

FC Zurich, Borussia Moenchengladbach of West Germany and Dynamo Kiev who, in the quarter-finals, had accounted for the reigning champions Bayern Munich. As luck would have it, Liverpool got the best of the draw in the shape of Zurich who were easily eliminated 6-1 on aggregate, while Borussia and Kiev fought out two mighty battles, with the Russians winning the first leg 1-0 only for Borussia to take the second 2-0 and so progress into the Final.

The game, which was played in Rome, was a magnificent affair. Even though Liverpool might have started as marginal favourites, the West Germans were certainly no lambs to the slaughter. Their side, captained by veteran international defender Berti Vogts, contained, in the likes of Bonhof, Wimmer and Heynkes, vastly-experienced West German

Simonsen (the best of the night) when he latched onto a misdirected pass and swept through the Liverpool defence before curling a shot round Clemence. From then on, however, it was all Liverpool. They resisted Borussia's pressure following the goal, scored through a Smith header direct from a corner and then put the issue beyond any doubt with a Neal penalty after Keegan had been fouled by a desperate German defence inside the area.

As European champions, Liverpool were back in 1978 in defence of their title, but without the services of Keegan, who had been transferred to SV Hamburg for £500,000 ($1,000,000) during the interim period. His replacement, costing £440,000 ($880,000), was Glasgow Celtic's Kenny Dalglish, in build and style not dissimilar to Keegan but without quite the latter's

caps, and in their diminutive winger Alan Simonsen of Denmark they had one of the best forward players in Europe—a fact underlined by Simonsen's 'European Player of the Year' award shortly after the Final.

Even allowing for the claims of the other 21 players on the pitch, however, the game belonged to just one man—Liverpool's Kevin Keegan. Although marked by Vogts (who had virtually shut Johan Cruyff out of the 1978 World Cup Final) Keegan had an inspired 90 minutes, tormenting not only his marker but on occasions the entire Borussia defence, which left huge gaps for Liverpool's midfield to exploit. McDermott put Liverpool one-up in the first half when he scored with an angled shot following Heighway's through ball, but Borussia equalized early in the second with a stupendous goal from

Above: **A fierce tackle is attempted by Poland's No. 6 during a 1972 international against West Germany. The Germans used their abundant** **skill and ability to run out winners. This was during the long period when they were undisputed world champions.**

vision and adaptability. He had survived the transition from the relatively slow pace of the Scottish First Division to the hurly-burly of the Football League well enough though, and had rewarded Liverpool's faith in him with 30 goals in his first season.

In their defence of the European Cup, Liverpool had a bye in the first round before being drawn with the useful East German side, Dynamo Dresden. Liverpool showed they had lost none of their power with a 5-0 win at Anfield, which effectively ended Dresden's interest, although they did salvage some pride with a 2-1 win in East Germany. In the quarter-finals, Benfica, not the force of old but still dangerous, were put out 6-2 on aggregate and in the semis, Liverpool came up against their old rivals Borussia Moenchengladbach. The first leg, played in West Germany, ended with an emphatic 3-1 win for Borussia and they approached the return leg at Anfield with understandable optimism. A lesser side than Liverpool might have felt the task in hand was hopeless, but the champions responded with a wonderful display that left them 3-0 winners and went through to the Final again.

Their opponents in that game played at Wembley were FC Bruges who had reached the Final impressively with wins over Kuopion Palloseura of Finland, Panathinaikos of Greece,

In 1979, Liverpool—as champions—were back again. The other English representatives were Nottingham Forest. Under the guidance of their charismatic manager Brian Clough, Forest had just scraped into Division 1 at the end of the 1976/7 season and then confounded everyone by winning the League championship in great style the following year. As ill-fortune would have it, Liverpool and Forest were drawn together in the very first round and after winning 2-0 in Nottingham, Forest managed to hang on for a goalless

Below: **In 1979, Nottingham Forest won the European Cup by beating Malmo 1–0 in Munich. As a Final, it wasn't particularly memorable, but it gave Tony Woodcock (red shirt) the chance to impress the watching Germans with his skills. His reward? A transfer to Cologne.**

Atletico Madrid and finally Juventus, overcoming a 1-0 first leg deficit and a *catenaccio* defence to win their home leg 2-0.

Sadly, the Final was a dismal and dreary affair. Bruges, deprived of the services of their talismanic veteran centre-forward Raoul Lambert through injury, eschewed the attractive attacking soccer that had served them so well on the way to the Final and fell back instead on blanket defence, seemingly content to hold Liverpool throughout normal play and extra time before chancing their arm on the penalty decider. Liverpool for their part performed well below par, but a solitary goal from Dalglish in the second half was sufficient to secure the European Cup for the second year running and save the spectators both at Wembley and in the world-wide television audience from the tedium of extra time.

draw at Anfield to send the European champions out of the tournament. After disposing of AEK Athens and Grasshoppers of Zurich, Forest found themselves paired with the West German champions FC Cologne in the semi-finals.

The first leg in Nottingham produced a 3-3 draw and few gave very much for Forest's chances of survival away from home. However, they turned in a splendid performance to win the second leg 1-0 and so reach the Final, which was played at the Olympic Stadium in Munich against Malmo FF of Sweden.

Malmo came to the Final with an extraordinary defensive record. In their ties with Monaco, Dynamo Kiev, Wisla Krakow of Poland, and FK Austria, they had conceded just three goals in a total of eight matches. Indeed, only

Krakow had been able to breach the Swedes' iron defence, winning the first leg in Poland 2-1 only to lose 4-1 in Malmo.

Against Malmo, Forest paraded their £1,000,000 ($2,000,000) forward Trevor Francis, the most expensive player in Britain. Fittingly perhaps, his was the only goal of the Final as dreary and negative as the previous year's had been, when he headed in a left-wing cross at the far post on the very stroke of half-time.

Across the Atlantic, the equivalent of the European Cup is the Copa Libertadores, a competition open to the top sides from all South American countries. In organization, the Copa Libertadores is very similar to the European Cup; the only major difference is that the tournament's early stages are in the form of qualifying groups, with the knock-out coming later in the competition. First introduced in 1960 as a direct result of the European Cup's popularity, the Copa Libertadores—like the European Cup—suffered some early teething problems, but really took off after Santos of Brazil (Pele and all) won in 1962 and 1963. To date, only Brazil, Uruguay, Argentina and Paraguay have supplied winning clubs, with Argentina being by far the most successful. Indeed in the last 11 years, the trophy has only left Argentina three times—to Nacional of Uruguay in 1971; Cruzeiro of Brazil in 1976; and Olimpia of Paraguay in 1979.

In the year that the Copa Libertadores began—1960—it was also decided that the winners of the competition would play the current European champions for what was termed the World Club Championship. Quirkily, although games are played on a home and away basis, aggregate scores were not used to decide the final result until 1969. Until then, a decider was played if the two previous games had ended in a win apiece—irrespective of whether the aggregate scores were level or not. Almost from the start, matches were marred by on-field violence, most notably those between Racing Club of Argentina and Celtic in 1967 and Estudiantes (another Argentinian side) and Manchester United a year later. In 1971, the then European Cup-holders Ajax declined to meet their South American counterparts, partly because they were worried about this continuing trend of on-pitch troubles

and also because they were unhappy about the political situation in Uruguay—the country they were scheduled to visit. In the end, Panathinaikos of Greece—runners-up to Ajax in the European Cup Final—stepped into the breach and played against the South American champions Nacional.

In 1972, Ajax agreed to play Independiente of Argentina and beat them 4-1 on aggregate in two ill-tempered games. The following year, soured by their experiences, Ajax stepped down again, so their place was taken by Juventus whom they had beaten in the European Final. In 1974, Bayern Munich refused to participate—their place was taken by Atletico Madrid—and in 1975 the competition wasn't held as Bayern and Independiente strangely could not find mutually agreeable dates. In 1976, however, Bayern did at last take part and beat Cruzeiro of Brazil 2-0 on aggregate. In 1977 and 1978

Below: **The 1978 European Super Cup, played between European Cup winners Liverpool and European Cup winners Anderlecht,** provided a rare taste of defeat for the English club, losing the first leg in Belgium 3-1 and then only winning 2-1 at Anfield. Here

Below: **Perhaps the best of Ajax's three successive European Cup wins in the Seventies was their second, a 2-0 win over Inter-Milan.** Both goals were scored by the mercurial Johan Cruyff, here seen receiving the attention of the dark-shirted Inter defenders.

Liverpool declined to take part in the competition. For their part, the South American champions have always put in an appearance, but the difference in temperament and playing styles between the teams of both continents has led to considerable problems both on and off the pitch. These in turn have led to the devaluation of a competition which should in theory provide a showcase of the very best team soccer in the world.

Perhaps marginally more meaningful is the recently-introduced European Super Cup, which was instigated in 1972 as almost a direct result of the continuing decline of the World Club Championship. The Super Cup is played annually between the current European Cup holders and the winners of Europe's number two tournament, the European Cup-Winners Cup—a competition for clubs who win their

Kenny Dalglish has an unsuccessful shot at goal during the first game.

Right: **The 1978 FA Cup Final** was won 1–0 by Ipswich. Here Arsenal's central defender **Willie Young** (yellow shirt) and Ipswich attacker **Paul Mariner** tussle for the ball.

respective country's knock-out trophy. Decided again on an aggregate, home-and-away basis, perhaps the most mortifying of all the ties was that between Liverpool and SV Hamburg for the 1977 Super Cup. After a 1-1 draw in Hamburg, Liverpool swamped their West German opponents 6-0 at Anfield, but what made the affair so piquant was the fact that in the period between winning the European Cup and meeting Hamburg, Liverpool had sold Kevin Keegen to the West German club. Keegan's feelings on being at the wrong end of a 7-1 aggregate scoreline at the hands of his old team-mates can easily be imagined!

Unlike the European Cup, no one club or country has particularly dominated the Cup-Winners Cup since it was first introduced in 1961. Indeed, only one club—Anderlecht of Belgium—has ever won the trophy more than once. Similar in scope is the third of Europe's international club tournaments, the UEFA (Union of European Football Associations) Cup, which is open to one or more of the top clubs not engaged in either of the other two competitions from each European country. Known as the European Fairs Cup when it was first introduced in 1955 (the name-change came in 1972), it has seen a majority of winners come from England (seven times to date) and Spain (six times). Lovers of soccer coincidences will delight in the two Finals in which Liverpool appeared and won. In 1973 they beat Borussia Moenchengladbach; in 1976, Bruges were the beaten finalists. When Liverpool won their two European Cups, the sides they beat were Borussia and Bruges.

No chapter on inter-club cup soccer would be complete without a mention of the most famous national tournament in the world—England's FA Cup. Countless words have been written about this great competition since its inception in 1871 because for some reason, FA Cup Finals crystallize the very essence of what knock-out cup soccer is all about—excitement, emotion, drama and achievement. Not only English followers of the game will remember the 'Matthews Final' of 1953 in which Blackpool's legendary winger Stanley Matthews turned in an inspired display to help his side with just moments of the game remaining, by turning a 2-3 deficit into an improbable 4-3 victory.

Well-remembered too is the 1973 Final between Leeds United, who were then one of the most powerful sides in Europe, and Second Division Sunderland. The result was 1-0 to the supposed no-hopers and few of those watching will forget their manager Bob Stokoe's rush across the pitch after the final whistle to embrace his goalkeeper Jim Montgomery, who had spent one of the busiest and most inspired afternoons of his life defying the Leeds attack.

Even the 1979 Final between Arsenal and Manchester United, though by no means a classic, still provided a typical twist in the tail. With 85 minutes gone, Arsenal were 2-0 up and cruising to a competent, though hardly electrifying, win. Then United scored twice in a minute, only for Arsenal to grab another and so run out 3-2 winners.

Right: **Exhilarating play in a European confrontation between Ipswich, from the English league, and Alkmar, from Sweden. Paul Mariner** **puts the finishing touches to scoring a goal.**

6

Soccer-US Style

The growth of the game in North America

Contrary to popular belief, soccer isn't a particularly new phenomenon in the USA, although it is certainly true to say that only over the past three or four years has the game achieved any sort of wide-spread national popularity and support. Soccer reached North America from Britain, aided in no small measure by European immigrants, towards the end of the last century. The game quickly established itself along the eastern seaboard of the United States, particularly in new Jersey, and in Canada too, which led to a US and a Canadian side meeting in 1886 in a three-game series. The following year, the countries met in three more matches, with eventual honours after the entire six-match series being equally divided with two wins, two draws and two defeats each.

In 1884, the American Football Association was founded and, retitled as the United States Football Association, it became affiliated to FIFA in 1914. From its arrival in the States until the late 1960s, soccer was very much a minority sport to baseball and American football. In areas where there was sufficient interest to sustain them, leagues consisting almost entirely of teams made up of immigrant players went their own quiet way and although the game was played in colleges and universities too, it never really succeeded in catching on with a wider audience.

This didn't prevent the USA from reaching three World Cup finals, however—in 1930, 1934 and 1950. In 1930, the American team, made up largely of former British professionals, beat Belgium and Paraguay to reach a semi-final against eventual runners-up Argentina who unsparingly whipped them 6-1. In 1934, the American demise was even swifter—an uncompromising 7-1 defeat at the hands of eventual world champions Italy. In 1950 though, the American team had its finest hour. Having qualified for the finals they found themselves facing the might of England in a small Brazilian town called Belo Horizonte. The England side, containing players like Alf Ramsey, Billy Wright and Tom Finney, were expected to run riot over the Americans, but instead they suffered one of those nightmare games in which they did everything but score. No such misfortunes for America, though—their centre-forward Gaetjens headed them in front after 37 minutes and that's the way the game finished: England 0 United States 1, the greatest upset world soccer has ever known. In fact, so unbelievable did this scoreline seem at the time that when it reached England by teleprinter, those reading the wire automatically assumed that there had been a misprint and that England had in fact scored 10! Though that defeat has been amply avenged on the subsequent sporadic occasions when the two countries have met, the memories of that extraordinary game in Brazil still rankle with English soccer followers.

Neither the United States nor Canada has since created the slightest ripple on the international soccer pond, but the signs are that this situation could change very rapidly over the next decade. In 1968, the North American Soccer League (NASL) was formed when two competing leagues merged. At the end of the first season's operation NASL was practically dead. Of the 17 competing clubs, 12 withdrew and that the remaining five agreed to keep going was due almost entirely to the unstinting efforts of Phil Woosnam, a former Football League player and Welsh international, who in his capacity as NASL's Commissioner encouraged, soothed, bullied and cajoled prospective franchise-holders, television companies, players and the rest to keep soccer as a viable entity in North America.

Slowly his efforts bore fruit. New York, Montreal and Toronto came into the League in 1971, followed in 1974 by the major West Coast clubs. Again due to NASL encouragement, soccer experienced a great swell of grassroots interest in schools and colleges and then finally took off with a

Previous page: **Flanked by cheerleaders—and quite happy about it—Franz Beckenbauer takes the field in Cosmos' colours. After a highly successful entry into the North American game in 1977, Beckenbauer sustained a serious leg injury that kept him out of the Cosmos side for long periods during 1979— one of the factors that contributed to a poor season for the New York team.**

Left: **All in a line, a moment of hesitation during a 1978 Cosmos versus Athletico Madrid in the US.**

Right above: **Action from Soccer Bowl 79. Vancouver's Willie Johnstone (no 20) gets** the better of the Tampa Bay defender Jan van der Veen prior to crossing. Vancouver —their side heavily weighted with seasoned British professionals—won 2–1 to take the Soccer Bowl for the first time in their history.

Right below: **More than living up to his name, Houston's Stewart Jump (no 13) climbs above Detroit's Angus Moffatt to clear an attack. Although he now plays his soccer Stateside, Jump has served with Stoke, Crystal Palace and Fulham in the English Football League, and is just one of a number of former English and Scottish League professionals who now play for NASL clubs.**

vengeance in 1975 when Pele was lured out of retirement by a three-year contract said to be in the region of $5,000,000 (£2,500,000) with the New York Cosmos. Pele's arrival in the US gave the game the boost it needed, for almost literally overnight soccer—or more particularly Pele—caught the public's imagination and League crowds of over 30,000 became a reality.

At the beginning of the 1979 season, NASL consisted of 24 clubs split into two Conferences—the American and the National. The 12 clubs in each Conference were further subdivided into three mini-leagues (Eastern, Central and Western) of four clubs each. Each team plays 30 matches during the course of a season, getting six points for a win, none for a defeat and a bonus point for each goal scored in the course of a game up to maximum of three per game. Therefore a winning side can gain a maximum nine points—a losing side a maximum of three. A draw is unknown in American soccer and their solution to games which do end all-square after 90 minutes could well provide a pointer to world soccer as a whole, where the normal answer to the problem of resolving draws lies with such artificialities as away goals counting 'double' and penalty kick deciders.

In the States, if a game ends all-square at the end of 90 minutes, a further 15 minutes of sudden-death extra time is played and whichever side scores first during this period wins the game. If the scores are still level after extra time, a novel form of tiebreaker known as the 'shootout' comes into operation, In its simplest terms, the shootout operates like this; a player from the away side has a free run at goal from a

mark 35 yards (35 metres) out. He is faced only by the opposing goalie who, within the rules of the game, has no restrictions on his movements. The shooter has five seconds in which to take his kick. If he misses, the goalie saves, or he takes longer than five seconds to shoot, the attempt is void. If he scores within five seconds, a goal is given. Each side has five attempts to score, each attempt being made by a different player. The team with the most goals out of five wins, but should both sides still be level after five attempts, then the shootout continues until one team or other misses. By placing the shooter and the goalie on a more or less equal footing, the shootout is an infinitely more satisfactory, fairer and more exciting way of settling drawn games and perhaps, given time, the method could be adopted as standard practice on a far wider basis than at present.

There is just one other area in which the American game differs from that played in the rest of the world. It concerns the basic Offside Law which states, as every soccer fan will know, that a player can be offside anywhere in his opponents' half. In an effort to encourage attacking soccer and provide more goals for spectators, NASL introduced their own version of the Offside Law in 1973. This amendment makes provision for all the usual offside principles *except* for the fact that a player can only be offside if he is within 35

Left: **One of American soccer's biggest captures has been Johan Cruyff, who in 1979 resisted the blandishments of the Cosmos** **and opted instead for Los Angeles Aztecs, where he rejoined Rinus Michels, his old guide and mentor from Ajax and Barcelona days.**

two teams in each mini-league plus the remaining two highest points-scorers overall from each Conference—a total of 16 sides in all—go forward to a knockout competition. Thus each Conference throws up its own champion and the two then meet in the early Autumn of each year in what is known as the Soccer Bowl—the nearest equivalent America has to the FA Cup Final.

Obviously with the number of sides actually competing in the NASL changing from year to year (from eight in 1972 to 24 in 1979), some Soccer Bowl victories have meant more than others. The 1979 champions were Vancouver Whitecaps, a team consisting almost solely of seasoned English professionals and managed by the ebullient former Blackpool and England goalkeeper Tony Waiters, who beat Tampa Bay

Above: **Action from a NASL game between Fort Lauderdale Strikers and the Cosmos. Cosmos' Dennis Tueart here gets the better of Strikers' Colin Fowles in this heading duel as the prolific Cosmos' goal-scorer Giorgio Chinaglia watches on, waiting for a deflection.**

Right: **Pele's last game. The match was between the Cosmos and Santos of Brazil —the great man's only other club throughout his long and illustrious career. Pele played one half for each side and is seen here in the Cosmos' change strip of dark green and white.**

yards (35 metres) of his opponents' goal. Known as the '35 Yard Rule' or the 'Blue Line Rule' (after blue lines marked on the field of play delineating the offside zones), this Americanization of one of soccer's most fundamental laws certainly did achieve its objective as regards attacking play and plenty of goals, but it brought problems for overseas players guesting for American clubs (who had to adjust to the 'new rule' and then adjust back to the 'old rule' on leaving American soccer) and also to the American international side which, when it plays in competitions like the World Cup or in friendlies against foreign international opposition, has to fall back into step with the Offside Law as it is interpreted everywhere else outside the USA. Sooner or later, of course, NASL will have to revert to the standard Offside Law (although there is a lobby in the States for the 35 Yard Rule to be adopted world-wide), and hopefully this will not prove too disruptive for the American game as a whole, or its players and spectators.

At the end of each American season, a rather complex play-off system is used to find the champion club. The top

Rowdies 2-1 in the Giants Stadium. It was the second successive Soccer Bowl defeat for the Rowdies and their likeable English coach Gordon Jago, for in 1978 they had fallen to the New York Cosmos.

The Cosmos' win in 1978 was one of the most impressive in the history of North American soccer. The champions in 1977, Cosmos won their 1978 mini-league (the Eastern Division of the National Conference) at a canter, winning 24 of their 30 games and scoring 88 goals in the process—a goals-per-game average which, if repeated in the English First Division, would result in the champion side scoring in the region of 120 goals. For comparative purposes, Liverpool scored 85 goals in 42 games during their 1978/9 championship run. In the play-offs, Cosmos had the mortifying experience

Above: **Yellow-shirted Philadelphia Fury defenders John Dempsey (no 5) and Brooks Cryder close down on Houston Hurricane's Finnish** **import Kai Haaskivi during this NASL game. Dempsey is now playing out his successful career, while Haaskivi is a NASL newcomer.**

of losing 9-2 away to the Minnesota Kicks, only to salvage an improbable shootout win in New York. Having duly recovered from this traumatic experience, Cosmos then won their Conference championship with an easy two-leg win over the Portland Timbers before beating the American Conference champions Tampa Bay 3-1 in Soccer Bowl 1978 which was played, rather unfairly, at the Cosmos home ground—the Giants Stadium in New Jersey.

While one can argue the toss over the suitability of this venue, there were sound commercial reasons for holding the game in New York. In 1977 when Cosmos won the overall championship by beating Seattle Sounders 2-1, the game was played on neutral territory at Portland in front of only 35,000 spectators. The 1976 Soccer Bowl attracted a mere 26,000 to Seattle to watch Toronto Metros beat Minnesota Kicks. Soccer Bowl 1978, however, drew a crowd of nearly 75,000 which was then the second-highest figure for a game between two domestic sides in the States.

Overall, the attendance figures during the season in the States are encouraging—the total attendance at games during the 1978 season topped the 5½ million mark, but for the first time in the 1970s, *average* attendances at games dropped during 1978—although only marginally—from 14,640 per game in 1977 to 14,046. As far as crowds go, easily the biggest

draw are the Cosmos—but only for their home games. In 1978, their lowest crowd still topped 32,000 while in each of their 17 other home games during that season attendances were over the 40,000 mark. Minnesota Kicks, San Jose Earthquakes, Seattle Sounders, Tampa Bay Rowdies and Vancouver Whitecaps all have good home attendance records, too— though none come anywhere near Cosmos in volume terms— but it has to be said that the picture elsewhere is bleaker (for example, Houston Hurricane draw only an average 5,000 home attendance to the massive Astrodome), and were soccer-crazy New York omitted from the statistics, the average attendance would be in the region of 8,000.

While it is unquestionably true that Pele's arrival on the scene in 1975 gave the NASL a boost that probably saved it from ultimate extinction, it also had one detrimental effect which still plagues the American game, namely the heavy reliance on foreign players at the expense of domestic talent. Pele (the only living person who can possibly rival Muhammad Ali's claim to the title of 'most famous human being on the entire planet earth') galvanized the American game. He became the player that everyone wanted to see and as a result attendances soared wherever he and Cosmos were playing. The other NASL clubs, while realizing that there was only one Pele, nevertheless came to the conclusion that if they too were to import 'name' foreign stars in quantity, they too would see their fortunes correspondingly lifted. So the great 'player drain' from Europe and, to a lesser extent, South America began.

Cosmos, keen to preserve their glamour image befitting a

club owned by showbiz moguls, bought Italian international centre-forward Giorgio Chinaglia (who has since repaid his transfer fee with interest, having score 68 goals in 73 games for Cosmos up to the start of the 1979 season, which is even better than the immortal Pele could manage—his tally in 56 games was 31 goals), Brazil's 1970 World Cup-winning captain Carlos Alberto, England international winger Dennis Tueart, Iran's 1978 World Cup team captain Eskandarian, and the great Johan Neeskens, in addition to Neeskens' Dutch compatriot Wim Rijsbergen and Brazil's Francisco Marinho. In 1977, with Pele in his last season and the need for a substitute star, Cosmos pulled off the coup of signing Franz Beckenbauer.

Elsewhere, Fort Lauderdale Strikers engaged Peru's Teofilio Cubillas and the goal-scoring talents of Gerd Muller. Los Angeles Aztecs signed Dutchman Wim Suurbier and then trumped the Cosmos by winning the signature of Johan Cruyff. Chicago Sting's swoop into Europe ended with Wim Van Hanegem and Sweden's Thomas Sjoberg . . . the list in full reads like a Who's Who of the great and near-great of recent years. 'Names' apart, there was also during the mid-1970s a big influx of English and Scottish League players who were loaned by their British clubs to NASL sides during the US season, which by a fortunate coincidence takes place during the British summer recess. At first, British team managers thought this a useful ploy to keep their players match-fit during the summer months, not to mention the welcome loan fees, but the increasing demands of the American game as its standards rose began to lead not only

to jaded performances when some of those on loan returned to Britain, but also the farcical situation in which to fulfil their contractual loan agreements in America, some players were having to miss often-vital end of season games in Britain.

This unsatisfactory state of affairs ended at the start of 1980. Now, any American club wishing to take on a British player must pay for his permanent transfer, but this in itself has created problems. Only a few clubs like Cosmos can afford the massive transfer fees that are now commonplace in Britain, so the wholesale export of British players to the States is bound to dwindle. This will have a long-term beneficial effect on the American game because hopefully it will force NASL teams to place more emphasis on the domestic talent available rather than the crowd-pulling appeal of big foreign stars. How the American soccer public will react to this remains to be seen, but although overseas players will still enter the American game, in years to come crowds in the States will perhaps get as much or greater pleasure from watching a home-bred American star as they do from a Pele, a Beckenbauer or a Cruyff.

The *current* reliance on overseas talent can be judged from NASL's own figures. Of the 574 players registered with NASL clubs at the beginning of the 1979 season, no fewer than 297 were non-US citizens—roughly 60%. On the coaching

Below: **Another of New York Cosmos' expensive signings, Francisco Marinho (white shirt) came from Brazil's 1974 World Cup side into** **North American soccer. Here he clears from Minnesota's Bjorn Nordqvist, himself a World Cup international with Sweden.**

side, the weighting in favour of overseas men was even stronger, with 20 out of 24 teams being in the hands of foreigners. When one examines the game in any other country in the world, the number of foreign players involved is tiny. Sooner or later, if America is interested in international competition, the number of foreign players allowed to any one club will have to be severely limited—as has been the case in Italy and Spain during recent years—even to the extent of placing a complete ban on the fresh transfer of foreign players into the States. NASL are clearly aware of this problem and are trying to combat it, but the solution may be a long-term one because as soccer's popularity is relatively new, the game is only now begininng to create a great swell of interest at grassroots level among schools and colleges. Already some of the young players that the American system produces are beginning to filter into the NASL sides—but many more are kept out by the presence of top foreigners. The time it will take for the States to establish themselves as a world soccer force will be an arduous period, as can be seen from the drubbing handed out by France to a largely young and largely experimental American national side in the summer of 1979. France won 6-0 at a canter, thus showing the present inexperience and inability of America at top international level. However, Americans have a reputation for being fast learners, so as their soccer tradition grows, so will their collective abilities—and there lies America's hope for the future.

Left: **Tampa Bay's Steve Wagerle (green shirt), bursts past New York's Franz Beckenbauer during the 1978 Soccer Bowl between the Rowdies and the Cosmos. The game, played before nearly 75,000 spectators in the Cosmos' Giants Stadium, ended in 3-1 defeat for the Rowdies and gave the Cosmos their third Soccer Bowl win and their second in successive years. Putting this defeat behind them, the Rowdies re-grouped and battled their way through to Soccer Bowl '79, only to experience the heartbreak of defeat again,** **this time at the hands of Vancouver Whitecaps, whose side, heavily based on seasoned British professionals, won 2-1. The Cosmos, deprived through injury of Franz Beckenbauer for the best part of the season, qualified for the playoffs from the Eastern Division of the National Conference, but missing 'Kaiser Franz's' influence, they weren't the force of '78. Despite a new influx of expensive foreign signings, the side did not perform well and were eliminated.**

7

Young Hopefuls

From school soccer to international–
the structure of the youth teams

look no further than the Brazilian game at its best, with its joyous attacking flair, dazzling individual skills and the almost inbred knowledge in the team that they have the capability of scoring more times than the opposition. In both cases, the actual ability of the players concerned is pretty much the same, which gives rise to the intriguing possibility that if an Italian side were to be coached by a Brazilian, the result might be Brazilian-style soccer, with the reverse being true if an Italian coach were given control of a Brazilian team.

This illustrates the importance of the coach's role in the modern game, for no player in his early formative stages is taught to be 'a defensive player' or 'a creative midfielder'— that all comes far, far later in his development. When a youngster begins to play soccer in school, he is, or should be,

For all the skills of today's current internationals, the future of the game rests more or less equally with young, up-and-coming players and with coaches. The importance of the latter in the game today cannot be overstated. Basically a coach, given a reasonable level of fitness and capability in his players, has a choice of adopting one of two playing styles, irrespective of any kind of tactical formation like 4-3-3 or 4-4-2. On the one hand, a coach can tell his team to play 'percentage soccer', keeping possession and waiting for the opposition to make mistakes; on the other, he may tell his players to go out and take the game to the opposition and so force them into errors. A typical example of the former is the Italian style of soccer which is cautious and, as some might allege, sterile and negative. As regards the latter, one need

Previous page: **Equalling the feats of their senior squad who won the World Cup in 1978, Argentina's youngsters tasted success in the second Junior World Cup finals, held in Japan in the summer of 1979, by beating Russia in the Final.**

Below: **Bob Latchford (white shirt, left) and Peter Barnes (white shirt, right) watch as Steve Coppell pounces on a loose ball inside the six yard box to score for England against Scotland, during this 1979 Home International**

Championship game which England won 3-1. Though both Barnes and Coppell have served England well, the increasing stature of Laurie Cunningham may mean that one or other will be sidelined in future England international sides.

Right: **A moment of confusion during the 1979 Junior World Cup held in Tokyo. Here the goalie dives away from a young USSR player with his Argentine marker in close attendance, closely watching the ball.**

taught the very basics of the game like the correct way to kick a ball, trapping, heading and so on. He plays the game simply because it's fun and he enjoys it and any coach who attempts to teach style or tactics to a beginner is courting the danger of killing off any love of soccer that the youngster might have. Once a youngster has mastered the basics, of course, come the finer points of the game and the introduction to a more competitive form of soccer.

Most European countries have school and youth soccer teams. In Britain, for example, an enormous number of tournaments are held annually for schools and youth teams. The most prestigious of these is the FA Youth Cup, which is open to any youth side but is always dominated by the junior squads of established Football League clubs, young professionals whose above-average fitness and skill gives them a marked advantage. From its inception in 1953, the FA Youth Cup was won five years in succession by Manchester United, whose youth policy was amply rewarded by the young immensely talented League side which was so tragically decimated at Munich in 1958. It has normally been the case that any club whose youth side wins the FA Youth Cup invariably does well at first team level a few years later.

If the FA Youth Cup is the most important competition for young players in Britain, the most established is the English Schools' Trophy, which was first competed for in 1905. Other top-grade tournaments for young players include the FA County Youth Cup, the English Schools Under 16 Championship and the Under 19 Schools Championship, all of which are extremely valuable breeding grounds for young players—although it must be said that in percentage terms the number of players who actually come through the full spectrum of schools and youth soccer to top-grade professional status is quite small, because while virtually all good young players have the potential to become good professionals, only those who can add dedication and discipline to their on-field skills have the right kind of mental attitude necessary to go to the very top.

Star professionals are rewarded with international appearances for their country, and the same applies for youth and school players. England field Under 15, Under 18, Youth and (at the higher end of the scale) Under 21 and Under 23 international sides. At the bottom end of the scale, the Under 15s enjoy quite a hectic programme during the course of each season. Their premier competition is the Victory Shield, a sort of schools version of the Home International championship—in which teams from England, Wales, Scotland, and Northern Ireland compete. Additionally, an Under 15 international player can also reasonably expect to play in a further three or four representative matches during the course of the season, either in friendlies against other European countries, or in a variety of fairly informal tournaments that are periodically held on the Continent.

Under 18s have a similar sort of schedule, including their own Home International championship called the Centenary Shield, together with games against foreign opposition. By the time they have reached their late teens and early twenties, most good young players have already been engaged by Football League sides and many are already established first

team players. In their transition from schools soccer to the extreme competition of the Football League, their international development becomes similarly affected. In theory, the stepping stones to a full international cap in Britain are Under 15, Under 18, Youth, Under 21 and Under 23 appearances. The systems in other European countries vary, but the aim is the same—a structure for young players to work their way up. In practice of course, a player's development never works out as smoothly. In fact, only one player—Terry Venables, formerly of Chelsea and Tottenham and now manager of Crystal Palace—has ever represented England at every single available grade of international from the schools side right up to full level.

The reasons for this are many. A player's mature ability

Left: **Arsenal's Liam Brady has the potential to develop into one of the finest midfield players of all time. It is a source of regret that in playing for the Republic of Ireland, Brady's full talents are never likely to be seen in their rightful setting of a World Cup's final stages.**

Below: **Nottingham Forest's Viv Anderson was the first ever black player to represent England at full international level. A fast and skilful defender, who also grabs a handful of more-than-useful** goals each season, Anderson is seen here on his international debut—England's 1–0 win over Czechoslovakia in 1978.

Right: **Brighton and Hove Albion's Mark Lawrenson (striped shirt) is rated as one of the best young central defenders in Europe. Along with O'Leary and Brady, he is a Republic of Ireland international, but injury held up his game during the 1979/80 season. Here he challenges Arsenal's Alan Sunderland.**

may not match his early promise or conversely a player may never catch the eye during his teens but really blossom in his twenties. His career may be hampered by injury or lack of application—the list can make long and depressing reading, for it is frustrating for a coach to put time and effort into the development of a promising youngster and then fail to see his efforts come to fruition through no real fault of his own.

That is not to say, however, that junior international soccer is inferior in any respect to the game as it is played at full international level. Indeed, on occasions in the bigger tournaments, the level of play is just as committed as in even the most vital World Cup game. More so perhaps, as to an extent many young players when representing their country's youth side feel that they are on trial as regards their international future.

The premier international event for these younger players is the Youth Tournament, now called the UEFA Youth Tournament, which has been held annually since 1948. It

has been won by England seven times since, with the victories in 1963 and 1964 providing a sound platform for England's 1966 World Cup success. However, as if to give weight to the theory that success at youth level does not *automatically* guarantee a shining future, England's unprecedented hat-trick of wins in the UEFA Youth Tournament in 1971/2/3 has yet to pass on its benefits to the full international side. Like their counterparts at all stages of international soccer, the youth side plays a number of fixtures each season in addition to the UEFA Youth Tournament although, perhaps strangely in view of the existence of the Victory and Centenary Shields, there is no equivalent 'Home International' championship at youth level in Britain.

The next step up from the Youth side is the Under 21 team, a comparatively recent innovation which provides a useful halfway stage between the Youth side and the more established Under 23 teams. As if to underline the importance of regular international play at this stage of a young player's

development, there is now a European Under 21 Championship, inaugurated in 1976 and played over a two-year cycle. The first tournament may possibly have heralded a future East European revival at full international level, for of the eight pre-quarter final qualifying groups, five were won by Eastern bloc countries and indeed only three—Rumania and (surprisingly) Poland and Russia—failed to qualify. In the two-legged quarter finals, East Germany beat Czechoslovakia, Yugoslavia accounted for Hungary despite losing their home leg, Bulgaria had the closest of wins over Denmark, while in the only all-West European tie, England did well to overcome Italy. The semi-finals, also over two legs, saw East Germany beat Bulgaria while England fell victims to Yugoslavia. The Final itself—yet another two-game affair—presented two fine matches between Yugoslavia and East Germany (in full international terms, both very much a second-ranked outfit at present). The first leg was played in Yugoslavia and was a rather dour affair. The Germans played blanket defensive soccer and were probably well-pleased with the result—a 1-0 win to the home side. The second leg was a cracker, with a final scoreline of 4-4 being enough to give Yugoslavia the trophy with a 5-4 aggregate win. As Yugoslavia followed this win in the inaugural European Under 21 Championship with a 1-0 win over Bulgaria in the Final of the 1979 UEFA Youth Tournament, it will be very interesting indeed to see how their full international side fares in the early 1980s.

As a result of the Under 21 Championship's success, the Under 23 team has lost some of its former importance, as the final stepping stone to the full international side for a young player is now the newly-resurrected 'B' side, a sort of England Second XI in which players on the brink of full international status can be quietly blooded without all the ballyhoo that so often surrounds a youngster who is plunged straight into the full international side. Of old, the 'B' team's function was to play matches against lesser soccer nations who would be severely embarrassed if faced by a full-strength side. Now its purpose is more constructive. The usual mix in the 'B' team is roughly half-a-dozen youngsters and a couple of players either currently in or on the fringes of the full international squad with the numbers made up by a sprinkling of seasoned campaigners from the Football League—perhaps past internationals—whose presence provides a valuable stabilizing influence. With an appearance in the 'B' team, an up-and-coming player can be virtually assured that getting a full cap is merely a matter of time and, from England's point of view, the fact that a player is gaining experience at open international level *without* the pressures associated with the full England side is a cause for future optimism. Certainly the arrival of Viv Anderson as a full international after a spell in the 'B' team—the first player in recent years to make the transition—means that the system is actually working as it was intended.

Anderson, of course, despite his orthodox advancement, is not the only bright young star on the British soccer horizon. In the 1979 England squad there were some six or seven players who should still be around at the time of the 1982 World Cup finals in Spain (always provided that England qualify) and beyond. Anderson is a fine defender, as has been mentioned, and his fellow full-back in England sides to

Left: **Built like a heavyweight boxer, but with a delicacy and one-touch skill not often found in a big man, West Bromwich Albion's Cyrille Regis soars above Chelsea's Steve Wicks to get in a header. Dual nationality enabled Regis to play for either England or France—he opted for England.**

Top: **In the summer of 1979, Ray Wilkins (red shirt) was transferred from Chelsea to Manchester Utd for £750,000 ($1,500,000)—a fair reflection on the stature of this young** **England international, who has swiftly established himself as a regular member of the England midfield since his debut in 1976.**

Above: **Ranking alongside Viv Anderson as a full-back of future international renown is Crystal Palace's Kenny Sansom. In appearance and style, the pair couldn't be less alike, but they could provide a perfect foil for each other once they have cemented their standing as full England internationals in future tournaments.**

come could well be Crystal Palace's Kenny Sansom, another outstanding young prospect.

In midfield, Manchester United's Ray Wilkins, who also made his mark at Youth and Under 23 level, is already an experienced full international with over 20 England caps to his name and is thought by some to be a future England captain. A newcomer to the England squad and sure to be a fixture in future years, is Tottenham's Glenn Hoddle who is yet another graduate of the England youth system. And a young midfielder on the brink of greater honours is West Bromwich Albion's Gary Owen, a more forceful player than either Wilkins or Hoddle, who could blend well with both in a 4-3-3 formation.

England has two forwards who each cost their present

clubs £1,000,000 ($2,000,000) in transfer fees and who both are still under 25. First is Trevor Francis, who early in 1979 left Birmingham City for Nottingham Forest; second is Laurie Cunningham (the second black player, after Viv Anderson, ever to represent England at full international level), who in the summer of 1979 left West Bromwich Albion for the legendary Real Madrid. 'El Negrito', as Cunningham is now known to his new fans, is a winger who, given the protection of referees, will strive in the Spanish game which is perhaps more suited to his fluid, graceful style than the English First Division. For all Cunningham's skills, however, he faces a battle royal before finally establishihg himself as an England regular. With wingers again back in favour under Ron Green-wood, the usual incumbents during 1979 were Peter Barnes—

other hand, though he does not have Barnes' mercurial qualities, is the more consistent of the two on a game-to-game basis and might conceivably be the better long-term prospect.

Apart from having three excellent young wingers to choose from, England is doubly fortunate in having equally good young players in the other forward positions. Tony Woodcock, now with the West German side FC Cologne after his transfer at the end of 1979 from Nottingham Forest, is just beginning to establish himself as a full international, while his departure from the 1979 European champions allowed a potentially lethal striking combination to develop at his old club between the million-pound man Trevor Francis and Gary Birtles. Francis, whose skills and goal-scoring abilities are well-known on both sides of the Atlantic, is already a good international player and well on his way to becoming an outstanding one. Birtles, now assured of a regular place with Forest after Woodcock's departure, is fast blossoming as a result and is already making encouraging progress—and scoring goals—with the England Under-21 side.

West Bromwich Albion's black centre-forward Cyrille Regis (who bears a startling resemblance to boxing's 'Smokin' Joe Frazier) is another for whom full international honours can't be too far away. Born in French Guyana, Regis could if he wished opt to play for the French national team and they would dearly love to have him, but the player values an England shirt more, despite the fiercer competition for honours, and is content to work his way through the junior qualifying stages before making his debut on the full international arena.

Of course there are many other fine young prospects in both the British and foreign games. Some will languish with an unfashionable club before bursting on to the international scene while others, for all their promise, will never quite make the grade on a permanent basis. Again, perhaps turning full circle, much depends on whoever coaches these young players to continually strive to improve their protégés' skills without in any way smothering them with a welter of tactical detail and also to keep morale high when success takes its time in coming. Coaches may be oft-maligned, but it is very largely in their hands that the game's future lies.

Left: **A touch of black magic from West Bromwich Albion's Laurie Cunningham as he tries a spectacular scissors kick during an English League match against Queens Park Rangers. In the summer of 1979, Cunningham was sold to Real Madrid for £1,000,000 ($2,000,000) and has already established himself in the Spanish First Division. Incidentally, this particular shot hit the bar and rebounded to safety.**

then of Manchester City, but signed by West Bromwich Albion as Cunningham's replacement—and Manchester United's Steve Coppell.

Barnes, the Professional Footballers' Association choice as 'Young Player of the Year' in 1976 has perhaps never quite fulfilled his extraordinary promise in the Football League, although he has scored some great goals. That he has pace and verve is undeniable and on his day he can be unstoppable, but he has yet to develop the knack of 'losing' a tight-marking defender, tending to rely on speed alone to lose a full-back which leaves him somewhat stymied when his opponent is equally fast. His game simply 'goes off' at times too, although in fairness to him, his performances for England have invariably left little to be desired. Steve Coppell, on the

8

The World's Greatest Team

A personal choice from today's top players

From the stars of tomorrow to the stars of today and a departure from the normal soccer book format. No look at the world game today can be complete without reference to its great figures but, as a result, it has become almost obligatory in books such as this to include 'pen pictures' on the likes of Pele, Cruyff and Beckenbauer to the extent that their career records and achievements within the game are now practically second knowledge to those with even a passing interest in soccer.

So, by way of a change, and hopefully to provide the reader with some thought and amusement, I have selected a 22-strong 'World Squad'—not from the greatest players of all time, but from those who have represented their countries at full international level over the past five years or so, and leave

it to the reader to play Team Manager and choose what he or she feels to be the best resulting side.

The breakdown of the squad is three goalkeepers, seven defenders, six midfielders and six forwards and the fact that I have limited myself to just a trio of goalies makes their selection the hardest of all, for the choice available is staggering. From England—Peter Shilton and Ray Clemence; Italy's Dino Zoff; Leao of Brazil; Sweden's Ronnie Hellstroem; Josef 'Sepp' Maier of West Germany; Ubaldo Fillol of Argentina; and Pat Jennings of Northern Ireland, who surely would have gained wider acceptance as one of the world's best had his country ever reached the final stages of the World Cup.

For a start, Ray Clemence would make my short-list. In addition to the goalie's standard attributes, he is also tremendously consistent. In Liverpool's 1979 Division 1 championship-winning run, he conceded just 16 goals in 42 games —easily a record low. Shilton, on the other hand, would not be short-listed, for fine keeper though he undoubtedly is, he has shown from time to time that in international games his

---

Previous page: **Austria's Hans Krankl pictured here playing for his country against West Germany in 1978. Krankl has beaten Rolf Russmann (no 4) for speed and has wrong-footed Manny Kaltz (no 5). In a brilliant performance, Krankl scored twice in Austria's 3–2 victory.**

Below: **England's Kevin Keegan, seen here playing for SV Hamburg, is the best player in Europe at present and quite possibly in the world. He was voted European Footballer of the Year in 1978 and 1979. Only Cruyff has also won this award twice running.**

temperament for the big occasion might be suspect. On England's 1979 European summer tour, for example, Shilton let in three goals in 39 minutes against an Austrian attack minus their star forward Hans Krankl and that's not the sort of goalkeeping lapse you would normally expect from a goalie of Shilton's quality. Of the remainder, I would regretfully discard Hellstroem and Fillol to leave Zoff, Leao, Maier and Jennings along with Clemence.

Leao is unquestionably one of the greatest goalkeepers ever to come out of South America and is a real veteran of the big occasion, having played for his country in two World Cup tournaments. If there is one flaw in his armoury, it is slight fallibility on crosses and as we are looking for as near perfection as it is possible to find in a goalkeeper, he too goes out of the reckoning. Of the remainder, Zoff and Maier have international reputations that are hard to equal. In the run-in to the 1974 World Cup, Zoff played 1,143 minutes of international soccer for Italy (the equivalent of slightly over 12 games) without conceding a goal, while Maier was the ever-reliable last line of defence behind West Germany's European Championship win in 1972 and World Cup victory in 1974 in addition to helping Bayern Munich to their hat-trick of European Cup triumphs. As for Pat Jennings, he is the only man

ever to win the Football Writers' 'Footballer of the Year' award and the Professional Footballers' Association 'Player of the Year' award in the same season—an honour accorded him in 1973 which was a tribute to his skill and popularity on both sides of the game. However, despite a record 60-odd international caps for Northern Ireland, he has never—through no fault of his own—been subjected to the kind of top-level pressures that have been part and parcel of the careers of Clemence, Zoff and Maier—so those three earn my vote as 'World's Best Goalkeepers'.

The seven defenders are thankfully slightly easier to choose, as four of the players involved are automatic selections—Berti Vogts, Paul Breitner and Franz Beckenbauer of Germany and Holland's Rudi Krol. The first three represent three-quarters of West Germany's back four during the 1974 World Cup, the absentee here being the rugged George Schwarzenbeck, a tough and experienced defender but without the skill and flair of Krol. The appearance of Beckenbauer in the back four might not go down well with those who regard 'Kaiser Franz' as more of a defensive midfielder, but although it was certainly as a midfielder that he began his international career, during his greatest years with West Germany and Bayern Munich he was ostensibly a back four player, although in his role of *libero* he would slightly play in front of the other three defenders.

As regards Vogts' inclusion, although there are many equally skilled full-backs in the game he gains my nomination simply because for so many years in the West German national side he was Beckenbauer's first lieutenant, covering

Below: **Few central defenders today have the talent and enormous depth of experience of Holland's Rudi Krol (left). He took over the national captaincy from Johan Cruyff** **after 1974 and helped guide the team to its second successive Final. Here, Krol shows he has pace in addition to aerial power as he heads Argentina's Leopoldo Luque.**

the gaps left when Beckenbauer made one of his surging runs upfield in addition to being the player to take up a close-marking role during a game when the circumstances demanded. True, Kevin Keegan gave him a very rough ride during the 1977 European Cup Final, but then Kevin Keegan is the type of player who on his best form, as he was on that particularly memorable night, would create problems for any defender. Better to hark back to the 1974 World Cup Final, when Vogts completely shut Johan Cruyff out of the game.

Paul Breitner is quite simply the best left-back of modern times, a perfect combination of tackling ability and attacking inclinations both welded to an ice-cold temperament. For a defender, Breitner was also a prolific goalscorer, though none of his efforts was more valuable than the penalty which levelled the scores at 1-1 prior to West Germany's defeat of Holland in 1974. After that World Cup, Breitner was transferred from Bayern Munich to Real Madrid where he was used in midfield, a tribute to his versatility in addition to his creative abilities. Rudi Krol has few peers as a central defender in the modern mould. A World Cup veteran with Holland and also a member of Ajax's European Cup-winning sides of 1972 and 1973, he now captains his country and although his career is drawing to a close, he is sure to be remembered as one of the best players in his position of all time.

Of the remaining three defensive places, next must come Argentina's World Cup-winning captain Daniel Passarella who had a magnificent tournament; he was inspirational to the rest of his team and superbly effective in his central defensive position. Place number six goes to Francisco Marinho of Brazil—a great left-sided defender from a country more renowned for the quality of her attackers. Along with Breitner, Marinho was one of 1974's most outstanding defenders and, like Breitner, he is a great lover of attacking runs down the wing. Surprisingly, in view of the continued success he would have undoubtedly enjoyed with Brazil, Marinho instead chose to follow Pele to the New York Cosmos, where he has helped the club become one of the most dominant forces in American soccer. The final spot in defence goes to yet another Dutchman—Wim Suurbier, a brilliant right-back who won European Cup honours in all three Ajax triumphs before seeking pastures new with Schalke 04 in the West German *Bundesligia*; Metz of the French First Division and now Los Angeles Aztecs, where he has teamed up again with Johan Cruyff and Rinus Michels. Suurbier won his first Dutch cap as long ago as 1966, but was as good as ever in defence during the World Cup finals of 1978.

The 'Magnificent Seven' in defence then: Beckenbauer, Vogts, Breitner, Krol, Passarella, Marinho and Suurbier.

On now to the midfield placings where the choice is again bewilderingly wide but where, conveniently, six players virtually select themselves—three of them are ball-winners and three are more in the way of creative play-makers. To deal first with the play-makers, an automatic choice must be another member of Argentina's 1978 side—Osvaldo Ardiles, who was unquestionably the best right-sided midfield player on view during that World Cup tournament. Never has a man looked less like a world-class player than Ardiles; diminutive and spindly-legged, he seems

to float through games, riding tackles with effortless ease and—needless to say—is a superb passer of the ball. In the late summer of 1978, he was transferred from his Argentinian club Huracan to Tottenham Hotspur for a bargain £360,000 ($700,000) and during his first full season in England, he defied his critics who maintained that he simply would not be able to stand the pace and pressure of the English game by effortlessly adjusting his style and adding a tougher edge to his play, all of which made him a more rounded and complete player. It is unfortunate that in moving to a comparatively mediocre side like Tottenham, he does not have the players around him to take the best advantage of his brilliant skills, but playing in the best company, he is, simply, the best there is.

Not far behind Ardiles in terms of creativity is Italy's Franco Causio who, like Ardiles, is a right-sided player. Causio's talents, when playing for Italy and for his club Juventus are often wasted. He plays in a rather withdrawn midfield role, but when he comes forward he is a player of great vision. Playing for Italy against England in a World Cup qualifier in 1976, he manufactured his country's opening goal with a cheeky little back-heeled flick which completely wrong-footed the England defence and laid the way open for the goal chance.

The third midfield creator's place goes to Trevor Brooking of England, a left-sided player who—like his predecessor for England and West Ham, Martin Peters—is a midfielder adept at the most delightful touches in the game in addition to having the perception and ability to throw a pass of some 30 yards (30 metres) that can split even the best-organized of defences. Like all players of real class, Brooking never seems flustered or hurried in his movements and he is also one of the cleanest and least temperamental of players ever to grace the game.

With Ardiles, Causio and Brooking to create moves, what better support could they ask for in midfield than three ball-winners like Romeo Benetti of Italy and the Dutch pair of Johan Neeskens and Arie Haan? In the way that Vogts and Beckenbauer blended together for West Germany, so too did Causio and Benetti for Italy, and also for Juventus before Benetti moved to play out the remainder of his career with Roma. Benetti is something of a hard man, frequently in trouble with referees, but he is nevertheless a real power-house in midfield when the going gets tough. He is also a

Above: **In a pose familiar to all British soccer fans, Trevor Brooking, seen here in the claret and blue strip of his club West Ham, passes the ball forward with his marvellously skilled and accurate left foot, in a League game against Southampton.**

Far left: **Reckoned by most to be the best right-sided midfield player during the 1978 World Cup, Argentina's diminutive Osvaldo Ardiles (striped shirt) took off to seek his fortunes in English soccer after the victory over** **Holland and, adapting his game superbly, was an instant success.**

Left: **One of the finest left-wingers of recent years is Yugoslavia's Dragan Dzajic, seen here rounding a tackle from West Germany's Berti Vogts. Apart from a brief spell with the French club Bastia, Dzajic played some 600 games for Red Star Belgrade and scored not far short of 300 goals—a fair reflection of the pace, control and shooting ability that marked him as a player apart.**

player of no mean skill, as was amply demonstrated in the build-up to that Italian goal against England in 1976, for though the touch of brilliance was provided by Causio, it was Benetti who originally passed the ball to him before 'reading' his team-mate's intentions to move forward and take the flick before bursting into the England penalty area and laying on the cross for Bettega to score with a well-placed header.

The exploits of Haan and Neeskens speak for themselves. Both established themselves in the great Ajax side of the early 1970s and also in the Dutch national side when they were still youngsters. Both played in the 1974 and 1978 World Cup Finals and in the latter game they showed that although they were no longer club colleagues (Haan having gone to the Belgian side Anderlecht, while Neeskens was at the time with Barcelona before his move to New York Cosmos), they had lost little of their old understanding. They can both best be described as creative ball-winners and both also have fine goal-scoring records, as Neeskens showed in 1974 and Haan in 1978 with some spectacular efforts from long range.

With 16 of the 22 places in the squad now filled, the accent turns to attack. Let me confess straightaway there's no Pele in the side. It goes without saying that were I choosing a 'greatest side of all time', Pele would be an automatic selection, but as his international career with Brazil came to an end in 1971 after well over 100 appearances, he comes outside the scope of this particular squad. There are no such doubts, though, over Johan Cruyff—for my money, a better-*all round* player than Pele ever was.

As a teenager, Cruyff was in the Ajax side that lost the 1969 European Cup Final 4-1 to AC Milan, returning in triumph to the spectacular successes of 1971/2/3. European Footballer of the Year on an unprecedented three separate occasions, Cruyff won every honour the game has to offer—except the one he wanted most, a World Cup-winners medal. The story of the 1974 Final is well-documented, but a big reason for Holland's ultimate defeat was the superb close-marking of Cruyff by Berti Vogts who shadowed him doggedly throughout the game after that first traumatic moment when Cruyff was fouled in the penalty area—a foul that led to Holland's only goal. A man who can create as well as convert chances, Cruyff settled down into the Dutch captaincy after a temperamental early career and, together with his long-time mentor

and friend Rinus Michels, he welded the side into a near-perfect soccer unit. His goal-scoring exploits are legion, but few can have been better than the one that cemented Holland's place in the 1974 World Cup Final, a breathtaking full-speed volley taken not far below waist height, earning the Dutch a 2-0 win against Brazil.

Cruyff retired from first-class soccer in 1978 after a two-club career with Ajax and Barcelona, the latter having paid a reputed £1,000,000 ($2,000,000) for his services. However, a series of unsuccessful business ventures led to his return to the game in 1979 with the offer of a lucrative contract from Los Angeles Aztecs of the North American Soccer League—a decision of Cruyff's that led to New York Cosmos feeling less than pleased after they had entertained thoughts of fielding both Cruyff and Beckenbauer in the same team. While both clubs undoubtedly offered similar contracts, Cruyff's final decision was made all the easier by the fact that in joining the Aztecs, he would once again be teaming up with his old friend Rinus Michels and the prospect, more than any financial consideration, was to prove the deciding factor.

If Cruyff is an automatic choice for this squad, then so is Gerd Muller, who retired from international soccer after helping West Germany win the 1974 World Cup. Muller's international goal-scoring record of 68 in 62 games speaks for itself and not even Pele can come anywhere near to matching it. After his career with Bayern Munich ended, Muller followed the footsteps of so many by joining a NASL club (in his case the Fort Lauderdale Strikers, where he has teamed up with Peru's World Cup star Teofilio Cubillas), and needless to say he is still scoring goals.

Berth number three goes to Kevin Keegan, the European Footballer of the Year 1978, 1979, who enjoyed a sparkling career with Liverpool and was a champion again with SV Hamburg, the 1979 *Bundesligia* winners with whom he had a fairly uneasy first season before establishing a fine rapport with both management and colleagues. Always a good player, Keegan has blossomed into a great one since his move to Hamburg. He is adept in midfield but better as a forward, and at present is not far off the very peak of his career. If England are to emerge from the doldrums of the 1970s, Keegan is the man most likely to be leading the way.

In the Muller mould of centre-forward is Austria's Hans Krankl, another player who had a fine 1978 World Cup, scoring four goals including a last-minute scorcher that gave Austria a joyous 3-2 win over their age-old rivals West Germany. En route to Argentina, Krankl scored six times in the 9-0 qualifying win over Malta and helped his club Rapid Vienna to the runners-up position in the Austrian First Division before departing for Barcelona to help fill the gap left by Johan Cruyff. As if to add further proof to the belief that a good player can play in any team in any country, Krankl finished his first season with Barcelona as Spain's top scorer and notched what proved to be the game's winning goal in his side's marvellously entertaining 4-3 extra time win

Left: **For once, Argentina's prolific goal-scorer Leopoldo Luque (left) has lost out. The man on the ball is Holland's Arie Haan, whose career has to date spanned two World Cups. Haan has that rare ability of combining both ball-winning and creative skills in his game.**

Above: Italy's Romeo Benetti has a reputation for power, stamina and ruthless tackling, but for all his 'hard man' image, there is still a skilful and creative side to his game.

Right: Italy's Franco Causio (blue shirt) has beaten France's Michel Platini (white shirt, background), and now he has full-back Maxime Bossis guessing.

over Fortuna Dusseldorf in the 1979 European Cup-Winners Cup Final.

The penultimate place in the squad goes to Italy's gifted young striker Paolo Rossi, voted the 1978 World Cup's second-best player after Argentina's Mario Kempes. Rossi is something of an oddity in the Italian national side. Unlike the vast majority of the players usually in the squad, he is outside the Juventus-Torino axis and until recently played for Lanerossi Vicenza—a club in which he has a 25% share-holding. However when the club were relegated from the Italian First Division (or *Serie A*, as it is known), the club reluctantly agreed to sell him with the proviso that he did not join any of the country's big clubs. In the end, he went to Perugia, runners-up to AC Milan at the end of the 1979 season and the only club ever to go through an entire Italian League programme undefeated, having contrived to win 11 and draw an astonishing 19 of their 30 games. Still only 25 years old, Rossi is a delightfully skilled player who can only improve with age. With his best still to come and bearing in mind his attributes now, his future could prove formidably good.

The final spot in the squad goes to Yugoslavia's Dragan Dzajic, who scrapes selection by virtue of the fact that although his best years were the late 1960s and early 1970s, he represented his country in the 1974 World Cup finals. Argu-

ably, Dzajic was the finest left-winger of the post-war era, certainly on a par with Spain's Paco Gento—another who could reasonably lay claim to that title. A man with a murderous burst of speed and no mean shot, Dzajic more often than not lived up to the admiring compliment of 'Dzajic is magic' paid to him by a commentator during the 1968 European Nations Cup when he scored the goal that knocked England out in the semi-finals and then scored again in the 1-1 final draw with Italy. During the peak of his career, his club Red Star Belgrade were Yugoslavian champions four times in six years (including a hat-trick of wins), and Cup winners on three occasions, their success due in no small part to this real king of wingers.

So the final squad lines up like this:

Goalkeepers
Ray Clemence (*England*)
Sepp Maier (*West Germany*)
Dino Zoff (*Italy*)

Defenders
Franz Beckenbauer (*West Germany*)
Paul Breitner (*West Germany*)
Berti Vogts (*West Germany*)
Rudi Krol (*Holland*)
Wim Suurbier (*Holland*)
Daniel Passarella (*Argentina*)
Francisco Marinho (*Brazil*)

Midfield
Osvaldo Ardiles (*Argentina*)
Franco Causio (*Italy*)
Romeo Benetti (*Italy*)
Trevor Brooking (*England*)
Arie Haan (*Holland*)
Johan Neeskens (*Holland*)

Forwards
Johan Cruyff (*Holland*)
Gerd Muller (*West Germany*)
Kevin Keegan (*England*)
Paolo Rossi (*Italy*)
Hans Krankl (*Austria*)
Dragan Dzajic (*Yugoslavia*)

The best in the world? Perhaps so, despite some notable absentees. There is no Mario Kempes, for example—a great World Cup, but disappointing afterwards; no Rivelino or Dirceu of Brazil; no George Best—still an international in 1978, despite all his wayward exploits; and no Kenny Dalglish, the only player in Britain—apart from Clemence, Brooking and Keegan—who can at present claim to be anything near approaching world class. But I feel this squad would give anyone a run for his money—though actual 'team selection' is left to the reader. One last task is to choose a captain, which isn't easy as Zoff, Beckenbauer, Vogts, Krol, Passarella, Cruyff and Keegan have all skippered an international side. The obvious choice though must be Franz Beckenbauer because of his acknowledged genius in the role and the proven manner in which he can motivate a team.

Soccer Chronology

The development of soccer worldwide

Although soccer as we know it today was born in England during the latter part of the 19th century, the game's roots can be traced back considerably further. A form of soccer was known to the Chinese in 200 BC, and also to the Greeks and Romans. In 1314, King Edward II of England banned youngsters from playing soccer in the streets of London; writer Philip Stubbes in 1583 described the game as 'a devilishe pastime'; a student was expelled from Oxford University during 1666 for playing soccer; and the game is mentioned in two of Shakespeare's plays.

By the mid-1800s, a form of soccer was played at most English public schools, though most practised their own variations of the basic game. 1n 1848, however, representatives from the top schools and universities got together and drew up the first universally-recognized set of rules in an effort to standardize the game and so encourage competition. Although these rules made kicking and tripping an opponent legal and in other areas too bore scant resemblance to the game as it is played today, they did at least ensure that the game was the same throughout the country.

In 1857, Sheffield FC—the oldest soccer club in the world still in existence—was founded and as more and more clubs saw the light of day, it became clear that a body to administer them should be formed. This came about in 1863 with the setting-up of the Football Association, which welded together clubs all over the country under one central authority. The first Secretary of the FA was one Charles Alcock and it was he who provided the impetus for the first FA Cup competition which began in 1871 and had its Final played in 1872. In that same year, the first official international match was played. It was in Glasgow between England and Scotland and ended in a 0-0 draw.

Although soccer was now a popular majority sport all over Britain, the game was largely dominated by Southern clubs, all amateur in the strictest sense of the word, who frowned on any idea of a player being paid for participating. This went hard with the Northern clubs whose team members, invariably working men, could not afford to take the time off to play and train. In an effort to get round this problem, more and more clubs began to make illegal payments to players to compensate them for lost wages and this led, in 1885, to the legalization of professionalism. As 'under the counter' payments were so widespread, we shall probably never know

the identity of the first 'true' professional, but we can get an idea of what players received for their skills from the wages of one James Forrest who played for Blackburn Rovers at that time. He was payed 10 shillings ($1) per match. To ensure that the richer clubs did not entice players away from their poorer relations, there was a maximum allowable wage for players (a concept not abolished until 1961), which made for little transfer activity at the time because whichever team a man played for, he would receive exactly the same amount of money.

Hard on the heels of professionalism came the birth in 1888 of the Football League, the brainchild of a Scot called William McGregor who realized that the wages of professionals could only be met if clubs were assured a regular weekly income and that such an income could only come from well-attended competitive games between clubs. Consequently, 12 clubs played out the first season's competition and the League was won by Preston North End who also won the FA Cup, becoming the first of only four teams ever to achieve this 'double'.

The South was slow to adopt professionalism and until the end of the 19th century, both League and Cup were dominated by Northern sides. In 1892, in order to cope with the ever-increasing popularity of the League, a Second Division was formed and a year later, Arsenal—the first London side to embrace professionalism—were admitted to League competition.

By the turn of the century, the whole of Britain had adopted the principle of competitive professional soccer. The Scottish FA had been formed in 1873 and a Scottish League in 1891, while the Welsh and Irish—in 1876 and 1880 respectively—had also formed their own Football Associations, which led directly to the setting-up of the four-way Home International Championship in 1884.

Abroad, too, the game was beginning to spread. In 1879, the Boldspil Klub of Copenhagen was founded, and Haarlem FC of Holland was formed in 1899. Expatriate Englishmen living in Italy set up the famous AC Milan club and the influence of the British abroad can be judged from the fact that there is a Liverpool club in Uruguay, an Everton in Chile and, in honour of a tour made to that country in the late 1800s, a Corinthians in Brazil. In 1908, England sent an international side abroad for the first time, playing games in Austria, Hungary and Bohemia, but even though England was at this time the greatest soccer power on earth, she had already squandered the opportunity of becoming the biggest influence on the field of play, as well as administrative power.

England lost this golden opportunity in 1904 when FIFA (Federation of International Football Associations) was founded with Belgium, Denmark, France, Holland, Spain and Switzerland making up the original membership. True, England did join in 1906, only to resign in 1920 over the question of 'fraternizing' on the soccer field with her World War I foes. England rejoined in 1924 but resigned again in 1928, this time over the age-old issue of whether amateur players should be financially compensated for wages lost when playing soccer (England was against the idea). She did not finally re-enter FIFA again until 1946 when, having already missed three World Cups, her supposed domination of the world game rested largely in the minds of opponents alone.

While the rest of the world were adopting a modern approach to soccer, Britain went her own quiet insular way. In 1905, a sensation was caused by the first £1,000 ($2,000) transfer when Alf Common moved from Sunderland to Middlesborough. In 1908, the same year that an English professional side first ventured abroad, the Olympic Games were held in London and the soccer gold medal went to the United Kingdom. The popularity of the Football League competition increased to such an extent that in 1920 a Third Division was formed for Southern clubs, followed in 1921 by another Third Division, this time for Northern teams. The Offside Law, which stated that three men had to be between a player and the opposing goal-line at the moment a ball was passed (and which had been utilized by scheming defences to drastically reduce the number of goals scored), was altered in 1925 to state that two men was sufficient for a player to be onside in an effort to increase goals. This change in the rules was rewarded in the 1927/8 English season when

Left: **The France national team assemble for the obligatory team photograph before an international match. Of all the pre-game rituals, along with national anthems and presentations, this is the moment players hate most as it allows nerves to build and concentration lapses.**

Right: **Brazilian defender Toninho (yellow shirt) was one of the best in the 1978 World Cup. Here he challenges Julio Cardenosa of Spain during a Group 3 World Cup match in 1978 which ended in a sterile 0–0 draw and provided scant joy for either fans or players.**

Bill 'Dixie' Dean of Everton scored 60 League goals—a record that still stands.

In 1929, Scotland emerged from insularity to travel abroad for the first time, making a brief foray to Germany where they drew 1-1. In 1930, the Jules Rimet Trophy, the inaugural World Cup, was held in Uruguay and won by the host nation. Four years later, Italy were the new world champions and retained the trophy by winning again in 1938, the last World Cup before World War II.

In the aftermath of war came the steady decline of Britain as an international soccer power. In 1949, England were beaten by Eire at Goodison Park in Liverpool, so losing their unbeaten home record against foreign opposition, but this defeat paled into insignificance when Hungary became the first foreign side ever to win at Wembley, annihilating England 6-3 in 1953. The following year at the Nep Stadium in Budapest, England suffered the worst defeat in her history—before or since—losing to Hungary again, this time by 7-1.

Having rejoined FIFA in 1946, England took part in the 1950 World Cup in Brazil, only to lose 1-0 to the USA. In the 1954 competition, both England and Scotland qualified for the final stages, and although Scotland were slaughtered 7-0 by the then-reigning world champions Uruguay, England did at least get into the quarter-finals, only to lose 4-2, coincidentally to Uruguay again. In the World Cup finals of 1958, England, Scotland, Wales and Northern Ireland all qualified for the last 16, for the first and only time. Scotland were quite hopeless and finished bottom of their group; England were unluckily eliminated by Russia, but Northern Ireland and Wales made it into the quarter finals, the latter at the expense of the mighty Hungarians. In the quarter finals, Northern Ireland, severely weakened by injuries to key players, were beaten 4-0 by France, but Wales put up the show of their lives against the eventual winners Brazil and in the end lost by just 1-0, that goal coming from an unknown 17-year-old by the name of Pele. In 1962, Brazil retained their championship, but in 1966, it was England's turn to win world soccer's greatest prize, beating West Germany 4-2 after extra-time at Wembley Stadium.

Away from the world soccer scene, the European game during the 1950s and early 1960s was dominated by teams from the Iberian Peninsular. The European Cup was introduced in 1955 and won by Real Madrid. With typical shortsightedness, the Football League advised Chelsea—then the current English champions—not to enter, but the instant success and popularity of the competition led the following season to the appearance of Manchester United in the tournament and although Real won the second of their five successive victories, United reached the semi-finals, a feat they were to repeat the following year—1958—despite having their side decimated by the Munich Air Disaster. As a gesture of sympathy to Manchester United, the European Cup's organizers invited them to compete in the competition during the following season, despite the fact that they were not the English champions, but with shameful callousness, the Football League withdrew their entry, maintaining that only Wolverhampton—as champions—should be allowed to participate. So Real Madrid went on to win the European Cup five years running, to be followed as European champions for two successive years by the Portuguese side Benfica. The only hint of British success came in 1963 when Tottenham Hotspur (in 1961 the first English side during the 20th century to complete the League and Cup 'double') became the first British side to win a major European tournament by gaining victory in the European Cup-Winners Cup, beating Atletico Madrid 5-1 in the Final. As for the European Cup, Britain had to wait until 1967 when, in the wake of England's World Cup win, Celtic took the trophy to Scotland. In 1968, 10 years after Munich, Manchester United at last emerged as victors, beating Benfica in an emotional Final at Wembley, thanks largely to inspired displays from England's most popular-ever player Bobby Charlton and a young Irish winger called George Best.

In defence of the World Cup, England travelled to Mexico in 1970, only to lose a quarter final to West Germany before Brazil gained her third win in the competition, beating Italy in the Final. In 1974, West Germany finally triumphed on home soil before Argentina recorded her first-ever win in the tournament during 1978. Though on an international level, England, Scotland, Wales and Northern Ireland never achieved over-much during the 1970s, Scotland at least trumped England by qualifying for both the 1974 and 1978 World Cup finals, while Wales made it into the quarter finals of the 1976 European Championship. On a club level though, heady success was achieved with Liverpool winning the European Cup in 1977 and 1978, to be followed by Nottingham Forest in 1979. In the Cup-Winners Cup, Manchester City and Chelsea were the victors in 1970 and 1971 respectively, while Rangers took the trophy to Scotland in 1972. West Ham reached the Final in 1976, only to lose to Anderlecht of Belgium. In the UEFA Cup, Arsenal, Leeds, Tottenham and Liverpool all had wins during the 1970s.

Looking ahead, Spain will host the next World Cup finals in 1982 when the final stages will comprise 24 countries as opposed to 16 as has been the case almost since the very beginning of the competition. After Spain in 1982, will come Colombia in 1986, though grave doubts have been expressed over that country's capability to stage such a prestigious event. As for 1990, perhaps the USA will have progressed sufficiently to take her place on the world soccer stage.

Left: **The Olympic football stadium in Moscow.**

1848
The first universally-accepted rules of soccer drawn up.

1857
Sheffield FC—the oldest soccer club in the world still in existence—is formed.

1862
Notts County—the oldest Football League club still in existence—is formed.

1863
The Football Association founded.

1867
Queens Park FC—Scotland's oldest club—is formed.

1871
The FA Cup begins.

1872
The first FA Cup Final. Played at Kennington Oval, it is won by the Wanderers.

1872
The first international. Scotland and England draw 0-0 in Glasgow.

1873
The Scottish FA founded.

1876
The Welsh FA founded.

1878
The first-ever floodlit game is played in Sheffield.

1880
The Irish FA founded.

1882
England beat Ireland 13-0 —a score that is still a record in the Home International Championship.

1885
Professionalism legalised in England.

1885
In a Scottish Cup match, Arbroath beat Bon Accord 36-0. A record score for a first-class game in Britain.

1888
The Football League founded.

1889
Preston North End are the League's first winners. They also win the FA Cup.

1890
Irish League founded.

1891
Scottish League founded.

1892
The Second Division of the Football League founded.

1893
Professionalism legalised in Scotland.

1895
The FA Cup is stolen from a Birmingham shop. It is never found.

1897
Aston Villa become the second team to complete the League and Cup 'double'.

1900
German and Uruguayan FAs founded.

1904
FIFA (Federation of International Football Associations) founded.

1905
The first £1,000 ($2,000) transfer. Alf Common moves from Sunderland to Middlesbrough.

1906
England join FIFA.

1908
An England international team plays abroad for the first time.

1910
Scotland, Wales and Ireland join FIFA.

1916
The first South American Championships are held. Winners are Uruguay.

1918
French FA Cup first played for.

1919
French FA founded.

1920
British FAs resign from FIFA.

1920
Division Three (South) of the Football League is founded.

1921
Division Three (North) of the Football League is founded.

1923
The first FA Cup Final at Wembley. Bolton beat West Ham 2-0.

1924
British FAs rejoin FIFA.

1925
The Offside Law is changed.

1927
First radio broadcast of a game—Arsenal v Sheffield Utd.

1928
British FAs resign from FIFA.

1928

Dixie Dean scores a record 60 League goals in a season.

1928

The first £10,000 ($20,000) transfer. David Jack moves from Bolton to Arsenal.

1929

England lose for the first time abroad. Spain win 4-3 in Madrid.

1930

The first World Cup, held in Uruguay, Uruguay beat Argentina 4-2.

1934

The second World Cup, held in Italy, Italy beat Czechoslovakia 2-1.

1935

Ted Drake scores seven goals for Arsenal in a League game against Aston Villa. A Division One record.

1936

Joe Payne scores ten goals for Luton in a League game against Bristol Rovers. A Football League record.

1937

A British record crowd of 149,000 watch Scotland play England at Hampden Park in Glasgow.

1938

French Football League formed.

1938

The third World Cup, held in France, Italy beat Hungary 4-2.

1946

British FAs rejoin FIFA.

1949

Eire beat England at Goodison Park in Liverpool. The first foreign side to win in England.

1950

The fourth World Cup, held in Brazil, Uruguay beat Brazil 2-1 in final round robin match to gain victory.

1950

England enter World Cup for first time, but lose 1-0 to USA.

1953

England lose their unbeaten record at Wembley as Hungary win 6-3.

1954

Hungary beat England 7-1 in Budapest. England's heaviest-ever international defeat.

1954

The fifth World Cup, held in Switzerland. West Germany beat Hungary 3-2.

1954

UEFA (Union of European Football Association) founded.

1955

The European Cup and Inter-Cities Fairs Cup competitions begin.

1956

Starde De Reims is the first French team to reach the European Cup Final.

1956

Real Madrid win the European Cup—the first of five successive victories.

1958

The Munich Air Disaster. Eight Manchester United players are killed.

1958

The sixth World Cup, held in Sweden. Brazil beat Sweden 5-2. Juste Fontaine of France scores a record 13 goals during the competition's final stages.

1959

Billy Wright of England becomes the first-ever British player to record 100 international appearances.

1960

Russia win the first European championship, beating Yugoslavia 2-1.

1960

The Copa Libertadores begins in South America.

1960

The European Cup-Winners Cup begins.

1960

The Football League Cup begins.

1961

Tottenham Hotspur become the first English team this century to win the League and Cup 'double'.

1961

The maximum wage principle abolished.

1962

The seventh World Cup, held in Chile. Brazil beat Czechoslovakia 3-1.

1963

Tottenham Hotspur become the first British side ever to win a major European competition, gaining victory in the European Cup-Winners Cup.

S. MATTHEWS

1965

Stanley Matthews becomes the first soccer player to be knighted.

1965

Substitution allowed in Football League games.

1966

The eighth World Cup, held in England. England beat West Germany 4-2 after extra time. Geoff Hurst becomes the first man to score a hat-trick in a final.

1966

The first £100,000 ($200,000) transfer between British clubs. Alan Ball moves from Blackpool to Everton. (The first £100,000 ($200,000) player in Britain was Denis Law who moved from Torino to Manchester United in 1962.)

1967

Glasgow Celtic become the first British side to win the European Cup.

1968

Manchester United become the first English side to win the European Cup.

1968

The North American Soccer League is formed.

1970

The ninth World Cup, held in Mexico. Brazil beat Italy 4-1.

1971

Arsenal became only the fourth side ever to complete the League and Cup 'double'.

1971

Pele retires from international soccer after 111 games and 97 goals for Brazil.

1973

Bobby Moore sets a new record of 108 international appearances for England.

1974

The tenth World Cup, held in West Germany. West Germany beat Holland 2-1.

1974

Gerd Muller retires from international soccer after 62 games and 68 goals for West Germany.

1975

Pele emerges from retirement to join New York Cosmos.

1977

Liverpool become the second English side to win the European Cup.

1978

Liverpool retain the European Cup.

1978

The eleventh World Cup, held in Argentina. Argentina beat Holland 3-1 after extra time.

1978

Kenny Daglish sets a new Scottish international record with his 56th cap.

1979

Nottingham Forest become the third English side to win the European Cup.

1979

Johan Cruyff joins the Los Angeles Aztecs.

1979

The first £1,000,000 ($2,000,000) transfer between British clubs. Trevor Francis moves from Birmingham City to Nottingham Forest.

INDEX

ACKNOWLEDGMENTS

The publishers wish to thank the following individuals and organizations for their kind permission to reproduce the pictures in this book:
All-Sport 11 above, 44–45, 49, 78–79, (T. Duffy) 1, 45, 60–61, 92, (S. Powell) 30–31, 38, 50–51, 72, 74 left, 76; Colorsport 10–11, 17, 28 above, 35 above, 39, 53 above 55, 63, 64, 67, 75, 77, 84; Focus on Sports Inc. (M. Palmer) 64–65; Horstmüller 15 right, 24, 36, 43; Leo Mason 46–47, 62, 68–69; Harry Ormesher 2–3, 4–5, 20, 26–27, 52; Peter Robinson Endpapers 6, 13, 16, 21 above, 22, 42, 44, 48 above, 57, 82, 88, 90; Sport Agence Magazines 70–71, 73, 91; Sporting Pictures (UK) Ltd. 56–57; Syndication International Ltd. 8–9, 12, 14, 15 left, 18–19, 21 below, 23, 25, 28 below, 29, 32, 33, 34, 35 below, 36, 37, 40–41, 48 below, 53 below, 54, 56, 58–59, 65, 74 right, 80–81, 83, 84–85, 85, 86–87, 89; George Tiedmann/Sports Illustrated © 1979 Time Inc. 66.

PDO 80-06